Legacy

Legacy

Winston Hardegree

iUniverse, Inc.
New York Lincoln Shanghai

Legacy

Copyright © 2007 by T. Winston Hardegree

All rights reserved. No part of this book may be used or reproduced by any means, graphic, electronic, or mechanical, including photocopying, recording, taping or by any information storage retrieval system without the written permission of the publisher except in the case of brief quotations embodied in critical articles and reviews.

iUniverse books may be ordered through booksellers or by contacting:

iUniverse
2021 Pine Lake Road, Suite 100
Lincoln, NE 68512
www.iuniverse.com
1-800-Authors (1-800-288-4677)

Because of the dynamic nature of the Internet, any Web addresses or links contained in this book may have changed since publication and may no longer be valid.

The views expressed in this work are solely those of the author and do not necessarily reflect the views of the publisher, and the publisher hereby disclaims any responsibility for them.

ISBN: 978-0-595-47920-7 (pbk)
ISBN: 978-0-595-71443-8 (cloth)

Printed in the United States of America

To my loving family.

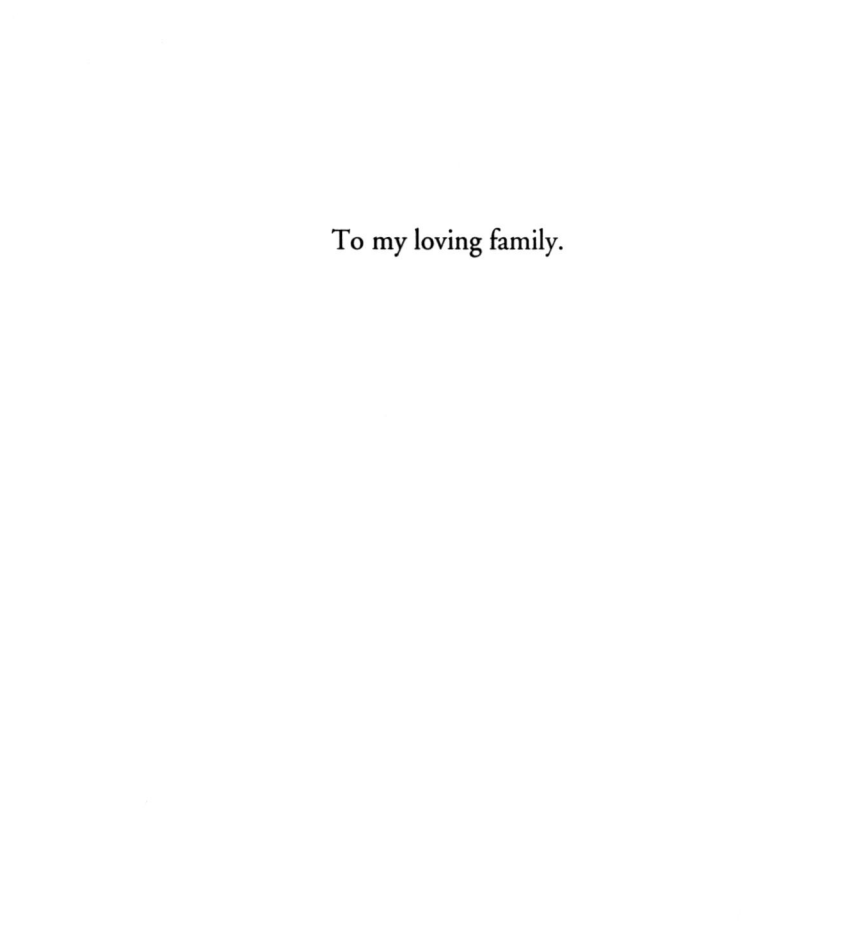

Contents

Acknowledgements xi
Foreword. xiii
Introduction xv
A Morning to Live For 1
The Blessed Earth Farm 4
When Autumn Comes 'Round 7
Blackberry Winter and Income Taxes 10
The Journey 13
The 'Possum Hunt 22
Good Guys and Bad Guys; and Snakes and Bugs and Lizards 29
Red-Tailed Hawks and Baby Chicks 33
Prom Night was Moonlight and Roses 36
Life and Love is More than Wine and Roses 39
I Guess We'll Just Finish the Trip Together 42
Miss Beth's Pasture Fence Garden. 45
Maggie, Big Boy and Tabby 49
Pepper. 53
A Mother's Day Rose 57
A Red Rose and a Hug and Father's Day. 60

Bob Edge, Rhododendrons and Sausage Biscuits 63
Don't Forget to Wash Behind Your Ears 66
Me and Jess and the Geezer Brigade. 69
The Bullfrog and Magical Gardens 72
A Wedding at The Blessed Earth Farm 75
Life's Way too Short to Hold Grudges. 78
I Was Finished With August on July 31stc 81
I'm Not Finished with October—Just Yet 84
Remembering Autumns Past 87
Beauty and Destruction: Joy and Despair 110
The Ludwicks: Super Volunteers 113
Our Beautiful Red Clay 116
I'm Surrounded by April 119
Daffodils 122
E.P. Todd Nature Center 125
Woody Ornamentals 129
The Queen of the Winter Garden 132
Pansies: The Jewels of Winter 135
Separated by Shadows 137
Kiss me at the Gate 143
The Little Tree That Could 146
Crape Myrtle 149
Two Little Rascals 152
Little Miracles Happen Every D 154
Traditions 157

Independence Day 2000 163
Knee Deep in May 166
Winter 170
Miss Beth and the Tree Wisteria 173
Sadie's Garden and Her Secret Mix 175
Birds in the Garden 178
Abraham Smith 181
Harmony of Change 187
The Alter of Change 190
Time 194
Epilogue 199
About the Author 207

Acknowledgements

Thank you to Beth Hardegree, my wife, for your love in health and in sickness, for your loving support while I wrote this book, and your help editing it.

Thank you to my many friends of the gardening community, who through the years have helped my passion of gardening thrive.

Thank you to my children, grandchildren, great-grandchildren, and dear friends who believed that this book was worth writing.

And, thanks to all of you, and many others, for the wonderful experiences of my life which provided the material for this book.

Special Thanks to my niece, Gina Palermo, for the original cover art and most of the photography in this book.

Loving gratitude to my daughter, Betsy Smith, for her work with the publisher in turning this from a manuscript to a published book.

Finally, thanks to iUniverse Publishing for their speedy processing, as they were aware of my heartfelt wishes to see this book in published form before my death.

Foreword

On a golden day in the autumn time of 1996, I heard three of the most dreadful words that a patient can hear from a doctor. "You have cancer." The bright golden autumn day made the words seem more ominous. Bad news should only come on dark and dreary days.

A week earlier my urologist had drawn blood to perform a PSA test. The test had come back with an off-the-chart reading of 48. An ultrasound and biopsy were ordered. Now, on this bright autumn day my doctor had called me into his office to deliver the results of these tests.

After he uttered the three dreadful words he also had to tell me that we had not caught the prostate cancer in its early stages. I can only blame myself for this. I had always thought that I was too busy to go for an annual checkup ... being too busy in this case may have cost me my life. As a matter of fact, until I realized that I had an enlarged prostate gland I hadn't seen a doctor for years. The doctor told me that the prostate cancer was pretty well advanced, and there was a good chance that cancer cells may have already broken out of the prostate gland. The prognosis was that we had a very serious situation on our hands—a life or death situation. The doctor suggested, and I agreed, that the best plan was to treat the cancer as aggressively as possible. It was his opinion that an immediate radical prostatectomy was the only reasonable treatment. We elected to go with the surgery, and the PSA returned to zero. The cancer was considered in remission.

Four years later, in 2001, the cancer was still in remission. I had finished several projects on which I had been working for the last six or seven years, and I began to look around for new project. For some time, I had been considering collecting my favorite essays into a book. I decided this would be my next endeavor.

Every three months, I was tested to determine if the cancer was still in remission. Some radiation and hormone deprivation treatments along the way managed to keep the cancer at rest. The success we had in keeping the cancer at bay led me to become somewhat nonchalant about the disease and about putting my book together. Procrastinators always feel they have plenty of time and tend to use words like nonchalant, instead of just plain lazy.

I'm not one to have worried much about the cancer anyway, since my philosophy always has been not to spend precious time worrying about problems over which I have no control. I knew that except for following doctors' orders and keeping a positive attitude, there was nothing I could do about the disease that had me in its grip. So, it would have been against all I had ever learned in life to worry about the cancer killing me, while I still had some living to do.

I was working sporadically on my book during this time, but I was still the perfect procrastinator: work on the book a few days and lay it aside for a few weeks.

Then in November of 2006 the other shoe hit the floor. I began to have severe pain in my left shoulder, and X-Rays showed metastasis of the prostate cancer to the bones in that area of my body. At least this time the bad news came on a dark and gloomy December day, instead of a bright autumn day. The weather didn't change the words, but somehow the news seemed more appropriate on a gloomy day. Likewise, I feel that funerals should always be held on rainy days—I'm a great believer in trying to keep the scenery in tune with the event.

Once again, the doctor prescribed the most aggressive possible treatment, and I took five months of chemotherapy and radiation treatments from January 2007 to May 2007—but to no avail. The cancer continued to spread, and the weapons were all used up. Admitting defeat, my doctor recommended that I enter the Hospice program.

During the chemotherapy and radiation treatments I was so sick, weak, and fatigued that I was unable to work on my book. Now, with a prognosis of about six months to live, I no longer have time for procrastination if I am to finish this book.

I'm now living my philosophy not to worry about a problem over which I have no control, and so far that conviction is rock solid. I'm at peace with the cancer and I accept that I am dying. But, suddenly, finishing this book has become very important to me.

My motive for wanting to complete and publish this collection of my writings is to share some of the thoughts and some of the stories that I've enjoyed writing during my lifetime with my children, grandchildren, great-grandchildren, the many friends, and some of the acquaintances I have made in my seventy-five years of a very active and diverse life.

I want this book to truly be a Legacy.

Introduction

Life lived forward is full of complexities, especially if it is lived on fast-forward the way I've lived most of my life. Life lived backwards is simple. It's like Monday morning quarterbacking, once you know how the play turned out you can't make a wrong call.

I'm now old enough to know how most of my plays have turned out, but I still wake up every morning eager to see what the new day will bring. I live life at a slower pace and more simply than I once did. The plays are less furious, but more meaningful.

This collection of essays includes many recent plays in my life, and some of the lessons I've learned from the older ones of long ago. I wouldn't dare disclose all of them—my grandkids might disown me—maybe my kids would too. But, my kids are now old enough to have made some of the same foolish mistakes I made, so they might understand and forgive me.

Almost all of these stories in some way reflect my journey to find a simple life in a complex society. I didn't know the words that Morrie Schwartz spoke in Mitch Albom's *Tuesdays with Morrie* when I left the corporate world at age fifty-six, in search of a less complicated and more satisfying life. In fact *Tuesdays with Morrie* hadn't even been written yet. But, had I known Morrie's wise words, they would have been my rallying cry.

Morrie Schwartz, Mitch Albom's old professor and mentor, is dying. Mitch, dissatisfied with the life he is living, but trapped by his own success, listens intently to Morrie's words: "… the culture we have does not make people feel good about themselves. We're teaching the wrong things. And you have to be strong enough to say if the culture doesn't work, don't buy it. Create your own. Most people can't do it. They're unhappier than I am—even in my current condition." Morrie's *current condition* was the last stages of ALS, one of the most horrible of diseases.

Like Mitch Albom, I was trapped by my own success in a life that had become abhorrent to me. I decided to change it when I was fifty-six. Looking back from the pedestal of seventy-five I wish I had had the courage to change my life much sooner.

My journey to create my own culture started nineteen years ago, when I decided it was time to simplify my life: to be finished with some of the things our culture was teaching, to be finished with the business of being a busy business executive. The thought that life was far too complicated and not nearly satisfying enough had nagged at me for several years, until I finally made the decision early one morning that the time had come to move on to other things—*to change my culture*. I'm one of the luckiest people alive, because I have been reasonably successful at this transition.

When I began my new life, I also began writing essays and short stories. Writing had always been one of my passions ... but one I had never had time to pursue as a member of the business race.

A very pretty lady was the catalyst for finally starting this book. Pretty ladies have been the reason for starting many things all throughout history—some good, some bad. Think Helen and the Trojan War and hundreds of other events down through the ages that involved the charms of our fairer sex.

She was in the Gibbs Cancer center waiting room one day—where I was waiting for my quarterly PSA test to be performed—and she kept glancing my way. It was summertime and she was dressed in a pink, raw-silk dress that fell gracefully from wide shoulder straps, and ended just above her knees. Her tall slender neck, long legs, and graceful shape reminded me of Audrey Hepburn. But, more than her physical beauty was the serenity, joy, and poise reflected in her demeanor. I must confess that even an old blade like me gets a little exited when a pretty lady keeps glancing in his direction.

After a while, she walked over to me and asked, "Aren't you Winston Hardegree?" I admitted that I was, and she told me that we had a mutual friend who had let her read some of my writings.

She smiled big and said, "Thank you, your writing warms my heart. I would love to read more of it." I told her that I wrote for my own entertainment and to sometimes share with friends and family. Just then, the nurse called my name, and I went in to see the doctor and forgot to ask her name. I couldn't see if her hair was dark like Audrey Hepburn's because, although she appeared to be not much older than Hepburn was when she played Eliza Doolittle in *My Fair Lady*, she was wearing a turban—the badge of a chemotherapy patient.

Her comment made my day. Knowing that my writing had brightened the day of someone who is facing the insidious disease of cancer and the debilitating treatment of chemotherapy—which, short-term, is sometimes worse than the disease itself—made me feel like my old comic book heroes. I felt like Superman, Batman, Captain Marvel, Flash Gordon and the Green Hornet all rolled into one. I sure hope she makes it through her treatments and becomes one of the survivors. I hope she's around a long enough to read this book—I hope I'm around long enough to finish it.

Prelude to *A Morning to Live For*

I've read and re-read hundreds of my writings trying to decide which should be the lead essay for this book. I finally decided on A Morning to Live For—*not because it is my favorite, nor do I think it is the best; my reason for selecting* A Morning to Live For *is that it best illustrates the simplicity and happiness Miss Beth and I have found living on The Blessed Earth Farm.*

There's much in these essays about how I set sail on a journey in 1988 to move from a hectic corporate life to simplicity and contentment ... as I believed life should be and wanted my *life to be. I wanted to move the center of my being from accumulating the trade goods of life, to accumulating what I had come to believe—at age fifty-six—to be the important things of life: peace, contentment, time to spend with family and friends, and time to observe and record the little things that constitute the real pleasures.*

Now that I know I'm dying of cancer and likely have only a few months left, I take great pleasure in reading some of the things I've written about the simple moments that Miss Beth and I have enjoyed on The Blessed Earth Farm. Already, I have physical limitations from the disease which prevent me from the blissful early morning walks with Miss Beth and our dogs as described in A Morning to Live For, *and in several other of the stories such as* Little Miracles Happen Every Day.

These physical limitations also keep me from gardening, which has always been one of my greatest pleasures ... and from many other activities that I miss so very much. I'm glad that I was able to record these experiences as they happened. I can now enjoy reading about them. I hope my friends, and especially my family will find pleasure in reading about my journey from a busy business executive to just a plain old geezer living a life of contentment, on a little farm in a remote area.

A Morning to Live For

Written Autumn 2002

Late last week we had one of those autumn mornings I live for. If I belonged to my grandchildren's generation, I would probably say it was "a morning to die for." I must confess though, that at my age I like the expression "a morning to live for" much better. The first real freeze and heavy frost of the season happened the night before, which set the scene for my morning to live for.

Miss Beth, my wife, and I sat around in the garden room reading the newspaper, drinking coffee and orange juice, and having our cereal and fresh fruit as we watched the eastern sky for the first hint of daylight.

As soon as it was light enough to see we donned our warm clothes and went out to the kennel to get our dogs, Spanky and Otis, to go for our morning romp through the woods and pastures of The Blessed Earth Farm. The last time I wrote about Otis and Spanky, I was still calling them puppies. They aren't puppies any longer, although on this fresh, cool morning they were acting like puppies, jumping, running around in circles, and ready to go. They'll soon be three years old, and they weigh about 75 pounds each. I used to say that they were real little gentlemen. They're still gentlemen, they just aren't little anymore.

They've quit chasing the cows and doing most of the other puppy things they did not so long ago. And most of the time they obey their commands, except for the *come* command when they are running free. This cold fall morning we put them on leads for the morning walk, or they would have been over in Greenville County before we could have turned around twice.

We also have a new puppy, Buster. He's about a year old according to our vet's best estimate. Buster was a stray that showed up out of the blue one morning a couple of months ago. He immediately stole our hearts. Even road weary and rail thin he had a character that said, "I want you to know that I'm independent, but I wouldn't mind a hand-out and a little help as long as you don't expect anything in return." This personality along with his devil-may-care attitude and his appealing looks made him irresistible.

Buster was already house broken, and we've made a house-dog out of him. It's the first time I've had a house-dog. I've always believed that a dog's place was outside. But, Miss Beth has taught me to love inside dogs—just as she taught me to love cats, which you'll read about when you get to "Maggie, Big Boy and Tabby." I guess you can still learn things at seventy, because I've sure learned to enjoy Buster's company in the house.

Buster loves to go for rides, but only in the big Ford Bronco where he can sit up high and survey his kingdom. He's not at all happy riding in the old Cadillac, and he even shuns Miss Beth's new Mercury. I think that hurts her feelings a little.

So on my morning to live for, Miss Beth and I, with Otis and Spanky on their leads, and Buster running free, stepped through the pasture gate down near the spring where the big white oaks grow. The red and brown leaves had about all fallen to the ground and we walked with the quietness of a ghost on the thick, soft carpet the leaves formed. We crossed the little stream and stepped into the frost white wonderland of the open pasture.

The frozen grass crunched beneath the thick soles of our hiking boots and the world stretched white with frost over the rolling hills of the pasture down to the woods of gold and red and burgundy and yellow. This has been one of the prettiest autumns I can remember, and the hickory trees have been especially pretty. There are many hickories in the woods of The Blessed Earth Farm and they have put on a show this year that would shame P.T. Barnum. There is one big hickory down by the barn that could truly be classified as a noble tree.

Our breath formed white clouds, and Otis and Spanky strained at their leads. When we came up over the first hill Buster was already playing with his friends: several little black calves that were born a few weeks ago and are just the right size for Buster to play with. I now know where the expression high-tailing it came from. As the black calves ran and romped with Buster they stuck their little tails straight up in the air and ran hell-bent-for-leather across the pasture. They were a sight to behold against the white grass.

There are few things which happen in my life that I wish would go on forever. My *morning to live for* was one of them.

Prelude to *The Blessed Earth Farm*

My late wife and I moved to Spartanburg in 1990 to care for two of our grandchildren who were five and seven at the time. Their mother, Mary, our daughter-in-law, had just died of cancer. She was only thirty-five. Our eldest son, Mike, had to frequently travel the Far East on business and was away from home for long periods of time. We built a house just a few blocks from Mike's house, and the children had bedrooms at our house just as they did at home.

I never could train myself to live in subdivisions, no matter how nice. So in order to satisfy my love for being outdoors—and for being able to walk and work the land—I bought a small farm about twenty miles from town. We continued to live in town; the little farm was just my special play pen. I spent time there growing vegetables, propagating woody ornamentals, and just generally loving the land. Some days I would go all day without seeing anyone. Other days neighbors would drop by to see me, and we'd sit under the big white oak trees drinking sweet tea, telling stories, and just talking the day away. I named the farm, The Blessed Earth Farm. The following essay conveys a little bit about my feelings during this time of my life.

I had no idea at the time I bought the farm what an important role it would play in the future of our family. I bought it to be my refuge. I couldn't possibly have conceived that the little farm and the old farm house would become so significant in the life of one of my children. I would never have believed what comfort the little farm would hold for me a few years later, when the greatest tragedy of my own life struck. But all these stories will be told in time.

I think my children thought I had lost my mind when I gave up the big house in town and moved to the farm shortly after their mother's death. I heard a few mutterings that weren't intended for my ears about why dad would want to live in that old house away down in the country, and the like. I think they probably thought that I would tire of this new life style, buy a nice big house and move back to town in a few months. The move to the farm was, however, one more step on the road to the simpler life I had been seeking for the last ten years. Sometimes it takes a long time to find your place.

The Blessed Earth Farm
Written Spring 2002

I've owned the land for about ten years now. I guess I should say the land has owned me. I paid for it, had it duly recorded down at the Spartanburg County Court House, and got a deed showing that it was mine to have and to hold forever—as long as I paid the taxes. I can pass it on to my heirs and I got lots of other rights provided in the legal jargon of the deed.

But, it didn't turn out that I owned the land. It turned out that the land owned me, and that the land had all the rights and the only rights it gave me were the rights to love it and to work it. That's all I wanted anyway. It has loved me right back, and has paid me abundantly for my labors in fresh vegetables, fresh fruit and in the beauty of the gardens.

For the first four years that I "owned" the farm, I traveled back and forth from my home on the west side of Spartanburg almost daily to work the land, a distance of about forty miles round-trip. There was an old house on the land. It was structurally sound, but it needed a face lift and a lot of tender loving care, which I was more than happy to provide. I would have loved to live there, but my wife liked the city; and our other responsibilities made it impractical for us to leave the town at that time. So, I postponed that dream until another time. Dreams often have to be put off for reality. But I still made the almost daily trip to work the land and, when the weather was inclement, to fix up the old house.

The next four years, I gave up my play pen to my daughter, Emily, who lived in the old house with her family. She used the front part of the house to start a jewelry design and manufacturing business. One side of the long front room was the office, and the other side was manufacturing and shipping. Today the very successful business occupies 14,000 square feet of modern manufacturing space in an industrial park on the west side of Spartanburg. Emily is not only a jewelry designer, but she has a decorator's touch, and she gave the house a nice face-lift while she was living there. She's also a very astute business woman, so under her guidance the business grew steadily, until she moved it to larger quarters.

The biggest tragedy of my life struck a few months before I came back to my farm. My first wife, Martha, died on my sixty-fifth birthday, April 4, 1997. A few months before she died, my son remarried thus relieving us of the responsibilities that had kept us in the city. After Martha's death there was no longer anything to keep me there; so in June of 1998, I moved myself and a very few personal possessions—my computer, about two hundred of my favorite books, a few of my favorite paintings, and clothes, toothbrush and razor—from town to The Blessed

Earth Farm. Emily's business had long before outgrown the farmhouse, but she still lived there, so we worked out a deal to swap houses and furniture, which saved us both a lot of moving.

I left all of the things that Martha and I had accumulated in our more than forty-six years of marriage in the good hands of my daughter, Emily, and started a new life. I no longer had things of the past to own me but I kept the memories, which would live on forever.

Material things have never been important in my life. I suspect that was one of the compelling reasons for my unhappiness with my old life. That life was based on accumulating wealth; I wanted a life that would make me feel good about myself. In Morrie's words *my culture did not make me feel good* and I wanted to see if I was man enough to radically change my lifestyle. But I didn't leave any of the memories behind; they're all still safely tucked away in my heart.

In September of 1998 I married Elizabeth Anita Sabin in a small ceremony under the big white oak trees at The Blessed Earth Farm. This event was another giant step on my way to the life of simplicity for which I was searching. Miss Beth loves the rural life and growing plants as much as I do, so The Blessed Earth Farm got a good deal, now it had two people to love it and work it. We got a good deal too—The Blessed Earth loves us right back—and we have each other to love.

Prelude to *When Autumn Comes 'Round*

Once upon a time, while living life on fast-forward, my ego was such that I thought that when it came time to write my autobiography it would take volumes to tell the story of my life. This didn't distinguish me from most of my friends who were also fast-forward executive types. We all had big egos and we all thought it would take volumes to tell about our mighty accomplishments in the business world as well as in our personal lives. My, how easily a reasonably intelligent man can let his ego get out of control and lead him down the fool's path.

Well, once upon a time is here. Recently, I found out just how inflated my ego had been back in those days. I was able to tell my life's story in 730 words—talk about a humbling experience.

When Autumn Comes 'Round *really tells of the essence of my life. All else is shadow boxing, but if you read the other essays that make up this book, you'll meet some nice people and some even nicer animals, and you'll walk the pastures and woods and streams and gardens of The Blessed Earth Farm with Miss Beth, our dogs, and me.*

July 30, 2007—I can now add a few words to my autobiography. Last Friday, July 27, 2007, my medical oncologist performed his final tests to check the status of my cancer. We now know that we are in the cold blue days of December (you'll understand this when you read the essay). All the tests show that the cancer has continued to spread. Alas, (I've always wanted to start a sentence with alas) the long days of suffering the side effects of chemotherapy and radiation were to no avail.

I think Miss Beth and I already knew what the results of the tests would be, but to have the doctor say the words, "We've done all that we can do. Hospice will keep you comfortable until the end," seems to add a finality that didn't quite exist before.

Now I try to wake up each morning and ask myself the question, "What can I do to make my life and the lives of those I love just a little bit better—in the time I have left and within my physical limitations, which already limit my movements considerably, and will limit me a bit more each day until my body will be bound to the bed or recliner.

When Autumn Comes 'Round *is my favorite of all my writings—with the possible exception of* The Journey.

WHEN AUTUMN COMES 'ROUND
Written Fall 2001

Last night I looked up at the big yellow harvest moon and it seemed that the old man in the moon was smiling at me alone, out of the billions of people on earth. I said, "Old man, I like your smile, but let's laugh together—we geezers have to hang together and laugh at the world or the world will overcome us."

Remember how you and I learned to crawl together back in the January of my life: you across the great field of stars and me across the pinewood floor of that old farmhouse at the foot of the great Appalachian Mountains. In February we learned to walk together and we prowled the far corners of the old farm. One night we walked out to the barnyard together so that I could see if the mules and cows really did sleep standing up.

When the March of my life came 'round we were running through the fields of the little farm hunting the night animals—'possums and 'coons—and in April we went courting together. Those were great days we spent together, back in my youth. But then, all of my days have been great, except for September.

In May we ran free and clear like a mountain stream, me across the great big world that I had found beyond the boundaries of that little farm in the shadow of the great Appalachian Mountains, and you across the indigo velvet curtain of your nighttime universe. In the June month of my life you worked your magic and brought me a bride, and you and I had to stop running for a while, because in July and August I was busy running with my children and didn't have much time for you.

Then September came round and the bride you brought me in June left to go and run with you in your great star spangled fields. I was sad in September and, as I sat and visited with you, I saw a tear of sympathy escape down the mountain of your cheek. In the September of my life I moved in a great circle and came out the other side. My career was finished, my mate was gone, and my children were running with their children. I sat watching the autumn storm clouds scurry across your face and fought the storm clouds that were scurrying across my soul. We knew grief and disappointment and uncertainty together. I was an almost old man, and for the first time in my life the way forward was not clear.

In the October month of my life I found a new bride and a new life. I came to live once again on a little farm not far removed from the great mountains. In October I looked at your harvest smile. It was kind of glowing and warm—like my soul these days. The autumn of life—like the autumn of the year—is good. It's bright blue and shining gold with a little storm thrown in once in a while to give me time to rest and reflect, and so that I don't get too complacent.

We've learned a lot together, you and me. We've learned to walk and run, to love and grieve, to have and lose, and I think I've finally learned what you've tried to teach me all these years—that I can't be the general manager of the universe. I still back slide once in a while, but mainly I'm content to let younger people do the managing these days.

Well, we've still got November and December to look forward to. I wonder what's out there for us. I know that in November your warm harvest glow begins to turn cool blue and by December it is as hard and cold as a blue white diamond. The experts tell me that even in the hardest blue white diamond there are warm lights, I've never been able to see them, but I'll believe the experts.

Maybe I'll discover the warm lights of your winter cold on a November Thanksgiving Day or in the bright star of Christmas. I know we'll still have the woods to walk, the cold creeks to cross and sweet ribbon cane to chew on as we sit by cornstalk fires in the night fields.

And finally January will roll round once more and you'll be watching as—somewhere—I learn to crawl and walk and run all over again.

Prelude to *Blackberry Winter and Income Taxes*

In June of 1998, I finally was able to move to my Blessed Earth Farm. In September of 1998 Beth Sabin and I married, and we decided to make the farm our home. Although she's a city gal, she loves the privacy of country living as much as I do.

Since 1988, when I made the decision to leave my old culture behind, until I moved to the farm in 1998, I had made good strides in seeking out the simple and more satisfying life I was determined to find. Moving to the farm was a big step toward my goal, and marrying Beth was another giant stride toward the goal. She jerks the bridle on my type-A personality when it begins to take over our lives.

Miss Beth and I had a small simple wedding under the big white oak trees in the back yard of the old farm house. Miss Beth decorated with some ferns and other plants and she rented some white chairs for the occasion. I set out a big tin wash tub full of ice, beer, wine and soft drinks. The guests for the wedding were a few close friends and family: less than forty people in all. The ceremony was simple and traditional. It was a warm September day and after the ceremony everyone enjoyed the shade of the trees while they visited and dipped into the tub. The preacher even had a beer.

We did complicate things a bit by renting a hall in the city—for later in the afternoon—and inviting a couple of hundred friends to join our celebration where we served some fancy food and had an open bar. We offset this complication, however, by requesting no wedding gifts on the invitations: we were trying to get rid of the clutter in our lives, not add more. Finally though, all was finished and it was Miss Beth, The Blessed Earth Farm, and me. We made a good threesome on our wedding day and we're still a good threesome.

Many of the stories, such as the one below, are about how Miss Beth and I continued to make progress toward our goal of creating a culture that was to our liking rather than a culture that is forced on us by the mores of society.

Blackberry Winter and Income Taxes
Written late Spring 2001

April 15th, income tax day, dawned cold and rainy. Miss Beth and I threw the household garbage in the pickup truck and hauled it down to the compactor station. That's one of the things you have to do when you live on a farm, but strangely enough, it's one of the chores I kind of enjoy.

The man that oversees the operation up at the compactor station said, "Looks like Blackberry Winter is here." I said, "Nope, I don't believe the blackberries are blooming yet." He's a nice man and he knows I'm supposed to know what I'm talking about where plants are concerned, so he told me that he guessed I was right.

Miss Beth and I stopped by the post office on our way home and mailed our annual donation to the folks up in Washington and the folks down in Columbia. That's another chore that I kind of enjoy. I'm always glad—in those years that I make enough money—to share with the government officials in Washington and Columbia. They always seem to be short of money.

We drove the pickup truck into the barnyard when we got home and Miss Beth and I decided to take our German shepherd, Pepper, for a long walk down through the woods, along the little creek, and back up through the pasture.

The rain had increased out of the northwest quarter and the wind was blowing sharply. The temperature had dropped down to the low forties. So Miss Beth and I donned old sweaters under our rain jackets and called Pepper to come on and let's go. Pepper doesn't need to be called twice when a walk through the woods and pasture is in the offering, especially on a cold rainy day.

A lot of people like to sit by the fire on a cold windy day, but Miss Beth and I enjoy walking the land when it's blustery and cold outside; and the nastier the day the better Pepper likes it. On a gray misty day the gardens always look fresh and sassy, and that gives my spirits a lift—especially on income tax day.

We walked down by the big spring and along the creek. As we crossed over the creek by the big spring, I noticed the watercress in the clear, still water was beginning to grow and that in the marshy area below the spring the tufted loosestrife was waking up after its winter nap.

In the woods the dogwood and native azalea were in bloom, and their blossoms sparkled through the misty rain like neon lights on Times Square. There is always something new to see when walking the land because of the change in seasons, and the changes in the light and shadows depending on the time of day, and time of year. We don't miss many days taking our walks across the land, and we always see something we haven't seen before.

The creek has cut a deep ravine through the land. We climbed up, out of the relative warmth of the ravine, although we were still protected from the wind as we walked up the backside of the big hill. But as we topped the hill, the northwest wind—now blowing hard—and the cold light rain that had started about the time we began our walk, blasted us full in the face. Miss Beth and I nestled our heads down into our rain jackets, but Pepper gave a little yelp of joy and went racing off to chase the cows—she was in her element and ready to run.

The grasses of the pasture were starting to green up. The tall fescue was beginning to grow nicely and the Bermuda and clover were showing signs of life. Some of the areas of the hillside are too rough for the bush hog to reach and that's were the black berry brambles grow. I looked at the brambles and saw dots of white here and there. The black berry bushes were blooming after all.

Next time we take the garbage up to the compactor station, I'll have to tell the man that he was right, but I know those blackberries weren't blooming the day before yesterday—I wouldn't have missed seeing something like that.

It's income tax day, it's cold and raining, and the blackberry brambles are starting to bloom. Miss Beth and I are back inside now where it's dry and warm, our cheeks are rosy and tingling as they begin to warm, and I'm feeling so exhilarated from the walk in the cold spring rain and wind that I don't even care that it's income tax day. After just finishing a big cup of hot chocolate I've started thinking about how pretty soon it'll be June and we'll be picking blackberries and making blackberry jam and blackberry ice cream. I'd be silly to waste my time thinking about all those folks up in Washington and down in Columbia, and how they don't spend my hard earned dollars as wisely as I wish they would: certainly when ripe blackberries are just around the corner.

Prelude to *The Journey*

My growing up years were spent between a cotton mill village and the little farm that was owned by my maternal grandparents, Mr. Willie and Miss Emily Tankersley. While my grandparents were living, I often visited the little farm. It was my one anchor in life that didn't change through the years. After my grandparents' deaths, I visited less and less often. I did, however, go and walk the land once in a while. It had been years since I had been there when I decided that I needed to make one more visit to the little farm and bring home all memories I had left there.

Growing up, I lived with my parents in the cotton mill village during the school term and with my grandparents while school was in recess during the summer months. A few weeks before school was out I would begin to pester my parents about taking me to the farm for the summer. I was good at pestering, because as soon as the last school bell rang my parents loaded me in their old 1930 Chevy and away we went.

I was lucky. I had two homes. One home with loving parents and one home with loving grandparents. When it was time for school bells to ring again at the end of summer my daddy had to come to the farm and lasso me in order to get me back to the mill village and to school. My momma always said I should have been born in 1832 instead of 1932 while there was still some frontier left in this great country. She thought I would have made a great frontiersman.

THE JOURNEY

Early Autumn 1992

The land has always been a part of me. I started my days on a small farm and it looks like that's where I'll end them up. In between, I lived in many worlds.

My maternal grandfather, John William Tankersley, or Mr. Willie, died in 1967. Until his death the small farm, where I started my days, was a place of permanence in an otherwise peripatetic life of fleeting glimpses. When the world was too much for me, no matter where in that world I might be, I would hop on an airplane and go back to Mr. Willie's place to rid myself of the shackles of civilization.

When Mr. Willie died the farm also died—only the memories remained. In 1990, two years after I quit the business of being a busy business executive, I found my own Mr. Willie's place. I named my place The Blessed Earth Farm. As I worked to establish my own little farm, I began to realize that Mr. Willie's place, the little farm of my youth, held my most abiding memories prisoner. I needed to go back there, unlock the prison and bring my memories home to make The Blessed Earth Farm my anchor for the rest of my life.

I started my journey on a hot day in August 1992, in the early cool just as the sun was beginning to streak the eastern sky with red and orange and purple. The journey was only three hundred miles in distance, but it was a lifetime in memories.

The great Interstate Highways took me from the Upstate of South Carolina to a place about half way between Atlanta and Birmingham. There I left the twin concrete ribbons of Interstate-20 and drove south along the eastern edge of the bottom of the Appalachian Mountains. Each road I turned onto was more narrow and twisting than the road before. Soon I was in a world that was stuck in the early twentieth century: a world not much different than it was when Alabama was first settled in the nineteenth century. Finally, I turned onto Clay County Highway 63 that would take me out to Cleveland's Cross Roads. About a mile down the road, along side the Primitive Baptist Church, I made my final turn onto a dirt road. This was the land of my ancestors.

I was home again.

I stopped my old Jeep Wrangler, turned off the air-conditioner, unzipped and removed the plastic windows, and let down the canvas top. I wanted to breathe the fresh air and feel the hot summer sun on my head and shoulders. I wanted to think about those long gone days when I followed a mule and plow, busting out furrows, as that same hot sunshine beat down on my head. The sun that shone down on the red hard-baked clay soil hadn't changed in all those years—the country hadn't changed much either.

Two miles further on down the dirt road, at the top of Goodwater Mountain I crossed the northern boundary of the almost four hundred acre farm that had belonged to my paternal grandparents Hugh Darrell and Rebecca Carroll Hardegree: where my daddy grew up. About three hundred yards past the mailbox I crossed the southern boundary line of their farm as I drove over the Clay County line into Tallapoosa County—the dust swirling up like a red tornado behind the

Jeep. On the right, just after the Tallapoosa County line began the four hundred acre farm that belonged to my Uncle Leroy and Aunt Willie Vee Futral.

My destination though, was seven miles further down the road to the small eighty-eight acre farm that belonged to my maternal grandparents John William and Emily Vernon Tankersley—or Maw Maw and Paw Paw, as I called them—where my momma grew up.

It's country where there are no chain stores—no CVS Pharmacies, no McDonald's, no Home Depots, no Wal-Marts, and no KMarts. I had left these behind when I exited Interstate-20 about sixty miles back, and wouldn't see them again until I reached Alexander City, Alabama, about twenty miles ahead. In this country it is sometimes miles between houses. It's a country where the kids still say yes sir and no sir, and address women as 'mam.

Here, there are only a few visual concessions to the modern world. The most noticeable are television satellite dishes standing like sentinels outside the shacks and farmhouses of the countryside. The concave dishes are painted with an elephant or a tiger—in the crimson and white colors of 'Bama or the burnt orange and blue colors of Auburn. The motto *Roll Tide* is painted below the elephants, and *War Eagle* is painted below the tigers. The satellite dishes, and telephone and electric lines are about the only visuals that distinguish this world in appearance from the world it was a hundred years ago.

Seven miles after crossing the county line I topped a hill and rolled onto land that had been the farm belonging to my maternal grandparents. I had intended to stop where the old house used to stand, but decided to ride on down the road a piece first. I wanted to get the feel of the land again before I faced my memories. At the southeastern corner of Mr. Willie and Miss Emily's place, the Cross Key Baptist church still stands. As a matter of fact, it has been enlarged and looks as though the congregation is prospering. Many years ago Mr. Willie donated to the all-black congregation the two acres on which the church was built. I understand it created a stir back in the days of the 1920s—a white man giving land for a black church to be built on the corner of his property in the middle of a white community was quite unconventional. Not many people, however, messed with Mr. Willie; he was a man who marched to his own drummer. I turned left at the church and drove about a mile down the road to Mr. Willie's daddy's place. The place that at one time belonged to my great-granddaddy, John R. Tankersley: where Mr. Willie grew up.

I pulled the old Jeep up next to the mailbox and looked for a few minutes at the dogtrot house that belonged to the man I only vaguely remembered. He died when I was about 5 years old. I remember him as an old man with a flowing white mustache and long white hair sitting by the fire in the house he had owned and lived in all of his adult life. The house was well preserved. Somebody with respect for the old houses of the world had done a first-class job of restoring it. I sat and looked for a while, then turned around and went back to Cross Key. A right turn would have taken me back to Mr. Willie's place, but on impulse I turned left toward New Providence Missionary Baptist Church, which was a couple of miles down the road. New Providence Missionary Baptist church was where my Maw Maw Tankersley and her daughters, Momma and my aunts, occasionally went to church. I never knew Mr. Willie to go. He wasn't much on going to church.

I wanted to see the church, not because of any memories I had of it, I was hardly ever there except once or twice a year for an *all day meeting and dinner on the grounds*, but because it is where most of the Tankersleys who lived their lives in the area are buried. The church looked prosperous. The sign out front was so new it looked like the paint might still be wet—it read:

New Providence Baptist Church
Since 1888
Bob Nelson, Pastor

Not Robert Nelson or Rev. Robert Nelson or Dr. Robert Nelson—but just plain Bob Nelson. I wondered what the old time hell-fire-and-brimstone preachers of my youth would think about just plain Bob Nelson out there on a sign in front of the church they had founded. I expect that they wouldn't find it formal enough or intimidating enough.

Instead of the neatly swept dirt churchyard I remembered from my youth, there was now a lawn. I looked over toward the cemetery and saw that it had been fenced with hog wire, and that along side the fence a big concrete slab had been poured and a basketball goal had been erected at each end of the concrete slab making an outdoor basketball court. I didn't much like the hog wire around the cemetery, but thought the basketball court was a pretty good idea. Kids running and shouting as they play along side the place where the dead are resting struck me as a pretty neat way to celebrate life and death.

Leaving the cemetery to investigate later, I walked around toward the rear of the church and saw that a new wing had been added, probably to use for Sunday school and socials. The new building was covered with vinyl siding and vinyl siding had been used to cover the aged wood siding of the original building. I guess that was somebody's way of dressing the place up. I would have scraped and painted. There's no building material as aesthetically satisfying as heart pine.

The foundation had been closed in, and some landscaping had been done. Central heat and air-conditioning had been added. I couldn't see inside, but I suspect they had also covered the old tongue-and-groove heart pine ceiling with some modern material like wallboard—will modern miracles never cease? (Sarcasm intended.)

Like Mr. Willie, I wasn't much on going to church, but on rare occasions Momma asked me to go with her and Maw Maw and my aunts, in such a way that I couldn't refuse. From these occasions I remembered a simple wooden building sitting about two feet off the ground on rock pillars. There was a pillar at each corner of the building and another in the middle of the two long sides where the floor beams were joined.

Cooling in the summer was provided by the shade of the big oak trees that overhung the building, the windows were opened wide to catch any natural breeze that might blow, and an artificial breeze was created by the women folk wielding funeral parlor fans at a furious pace. In the winter, heat was supplied by a well-stoked pot-bellied stove in the center of the thirty by fifty foot room.

I walked out of the shade of the churchyard into the hot sunshine and toward the graveyard. I got as far as the gate someone had built to get through the fence into the cemetery and it occurred to me that I ought to make a few notes while I was there—names, birthdays, and dates of deaths of some of the relatives—thus began my odyssey into family research. I walked back to the dust covered Jeep, got a legal pad and a couple of pencils out of my duffle bag, and returned to the cemetery. I made a lot of notes that morning as I walked among the grave markers. I counted one hundred and eighteen graves and thirty-three of them had gravestones that bore the name Tankersley.

I wrote down all the information on the Tankersleys—those I remembered and those I never knew. I wonder if any Tankersleys still attend this church. I don't think so, but I can imagine the congregation a few years from now, when the last of the old folks named Tankersley have died off, and no one remembers or knows a living Tankersley, looking out over that graveyard and wondering, "Who the hell were all these Tankersleys."

I moved back into the churchyard, and, after a long time in the August sun, the shade of the big trees felt good. I stood looking at the old church and could almost see it as it had been, in those times long ago, on a hot Sunday in August when an *all day meeting and dinner on the grounds* was being held. All day meetings were the only ones I would go to willingly. They were more like all day parties at most country churches.

My mind opened up to the past and I saw children playing tag and hide-and-seek, and young couples of courting age disappearing, hand-in-hand, into the woods. I saw the old men standing around whittling, chewing and spitting tobacco, shuffling their brogans in the sand, talking about the weather and their crops. They never looked directly at one another as they slyly laid the ground work for trading mules or pigs or cows or jack knives, during the next week, or the week after, or maybe the week after that—things important to old men. Time wasn't important to them. They lived in a world that operated on seasons and calendars instead of watches and appointment books.

The women folk were all inside helping with the singing and the praying, and hollering amen and hallelujah as the preacher preached the two thousand year old sermon of salvation as though it was a message that had just been handed down from on high yesterday. As they prayed and sang and hollered, they were busy moving the warm air around with the funeral parlor fans and casting holier-than-thou looks at one another—things important to old women. Time wasn't important to the women folks either. They lived in a world that operated on the time between babies and, if they lived long enough, the time between grandbabies.

I stood in the cool black spot made by the shade of the big trees, and once again heard the sound of gospel piano and of sacred-heart singing sifting through the open windows. I again saw and smelled all of that good food, especially the skillet-fried chicken, waiting to be eaten on the long wood tables—tables set up in the best place to catch the breeze and miss the sun. I could almost taste the fresh-squeezed lemonade with big hunks of icehouse ice floating around in the big tin tubs. And, I could hear the trickling of the nearby creek where the baptizing would take place later in the day.

Now-a-days, the air-conditioner is going full blast and all the activity takes place inside the church. The old women don't have to fan anymore, and the old men don't stand around outside whittling whistles for the children and chewing tobacco and spitting and talking crops. I wonder what's important to the old men and the old women now. The preacher standing in the pulpit now is just plain Bob Nelson. Fifty years ago he would have been the Right Reverend Robert James Nelson, and he wouldn't have been called Bob, but Brother Nelson or Preacher Nelson. And just plain Bob Nelson doesn't preach hell, fire, and brimstone the way Preacher Robert James Nelson would have—Bob preaches pop psychology.

The children don't play tag and hide-and-seek outdoors anymore, maybe a little basketball on the new court, but, like city children, they now stay inside on August meeting days and complain that it's too hot to play outside, and how long before we can go home to the television and the internet. The young couples, of courting age, don't come to all day meetings anymore—they have their own air-conditioned cars now and they go other places. And there's an indoor baptismal font where the water is not too hot and not too cold and new members being baptized into the church don't have to get mud between their toes getting in and out of the creek.

Are the changes good or bad? Have we gained or lost? I don't know—some gain, some loss, I suppose. But it seems to me we've given up a lot of good living for a lot of *things*.

I was in a pensive mood as I brushed the red dust off the driver's seat, climbed back in the Wrangler and drove the two miles back down the dusty road to Mr. Willie and Miss Emily's old homestead, where my memories were held prisoner. My meditative mood didn't alter as I stopped at the old farm, climbed out of the Jeep, and started to look for some sign of the old driveway that led from the road up to the house. The property has all been fenced in and turned into pasture for growing beef cattle now. Grass covers the rolling land that I remembered as fields of white cotton and tall green corn, strawberry and dewberry patches, long rows of vegetables, and all the other good things we worked so hard to cultivate. I remembered the rows that lay neat and weed free in the August months of years past.

I finally found the faint outline of the driveway, but only because I knew where to look. To a stranger it would have been completely obliterated by time and erosion. I climbed over the barbed wire fence, and walked slowly up the phantom driveway of yesterday to where the old house had once stood. I saw that the big pecan tree that had grown behind the house was still there and thriving.

All the buildings: the house, the smokehouse, the barn, the cotton house, the blacksmith shop, the well shelter, and the outhouse were gone. Recycled into the earth again, as all things eventually are. The only sign that this was once a home place was the skeleton of the old corncrib. It stood stark against the hot, blue-white August sky and would have fallen and rotted by now except for an Empress tree that grew up the south side of it. The tree was tall and strong enough to prop up the old crib. The batten boards fell off and rotted long ago. The strong frame of the old building will eventually rot and it will fall. As the wood composts it will provide food for the tree to grow. Nature doesn't waste anything. Even the old stone chimneys, usually the last sign of a home place, were gone. Someone probably decided they wanted the rocks for something else.

I walked up to an outcrop of boulders that marked the spot where the back porch of the house had been, and I stood for a long time on the parched grass. If

I had come in March instead of August the daffodils that had always been there would have had stuck their heads up and bloomed around the boulders. Daffodils are tough little plants, they continue to live and bloom their sunshine blossoms long after the people and their dreams and the buildings and the singing and the praying and the crying and the laughing are gone from an old home place. They show up year after year, keeping their hopeless, lonely vigil.

I stood, an almost old man, in the hot sun on the parched grass, but I was once again a barefoot boy. I was once again standing on the planks of the back porch scrubbed soft by the corn shuck mops wielded with energetic fury by Miss Emily every Friday afternoon. "Cleanliness is next to Godliness" was more than a proverb to her. I stood there, on the porch, and again saw her open the screen door, drying her hands on her apron as she walked through the door. She said, "Winston, aren't the daffodils pretty this year. Bring my bonnet and we'll pick a few for a bouquet to put on the table."

Looking on across the imaginary field of knee high corn I could see the *old man,* hand-to-the-plow-stock, shouting orders to the big red mule, "Whoa, Red. Gee-haw, come on 'git-up you lazy old mule".

The hens nested in the shed that was built onto the east side of the barn. I could hear them cackle, proud of the eggs they had just laid. I saw the corncrib crammed full to the rafters of new crop corn, the smokehouse with big succulent hams hanging from the rafters and the barn chocked full of newly cut hay. I could see the cedar shingle shelter that covered the well: a well with water so cold and clear and sweet that I can still taste it fifty-five years later as I stand on the parched grass beneath the Alabama summer sky.

I walked down through the field of tall green corn. I didn't see the pasture that it had become. Today it was still the cornfield of my youth. I walked on down to the big red cedar that had been my magic place when I was a boy. It was the place where I took all my troubles and hurts and problems, and there in the shade and the cool, sitting on the carpet of soft needles under the big tree, I licked my wounds, solved my problems, cured my hurts, forgot my troubles, and returned to my world happy and productive again.

I walked back to where the house and all the good times used to be, reluctantly opened the door to the Jeep, got in and drove away—back up the dirt roads, to the asphalt roads, and on up the main highway to Interstate-20. It was long after dark when I saw the bright lights of the Atlanta skyline. I drove through the busy downtown of the great city, picked up Interstate-85, and left the bright lights of Atlanta behind as I drove into the dark toward South Carolina and the future. I had unlocked my memories and brought them home with me.

Mr. Willie's place is gone, but now it lives on at The Blessed Earth Farm. I had finally picked up the anchor, the one thing that had remained constant all my life, and moved it to the place where it will remain the lasting constant in my life.

Prelude to *The 'Possum Hunt*

Not many boys are privileged to have a grandfather like my maternal grandfather, John William Tankersley. I called him Paw Paw, as did his other twenty-one grand children. He was known to his friends and in the community as Mr. Willie. He was a tall strong man who marched to his own drummer. He was always ready to help a neighbor in need, and he loved to play his fiddle for square dances, but other than that he didn't socialize much.

I had a wonderful father who was one of the kindest, gentlest men I have ever known. He spent a lot of time with me, but he was so in love with my mother that most of his spare time was spent with her. My father loved us, but he was no outdoorsman, and his time spent with my mother allowed me to spend a lot of time with Mr. Willie. This was fine by me, since we both loved the outdoors things in life. My brother didn't care for hunting and digging in the dirt and other outdoor things, so he was closer to my father.

Mr. Willie believed in a balance of work and play. Work was plowing, planting, and harvesting in order to eat. He probably never had more than five hundred dollars at one time in his life, but through hard work he produced enough food for his wife, himself and seven children; and anyone that happened to be around at meal time was welcome to put their feet under the table.

I enjoyed working with him, and he taught me to plow a mule and a lot of other things about farming. His idea of play suited me too. Skinny-dipping in the creek, fishing for food, and hunting small game: squirrel, rabbit and 'possum—all of which we ate. 'Possum hunting was the men's play period; women didn't get to go 'possum hunting.

This essay tells of my first 'possum hunt with the old man, which also was my initiation into manhood, although I didn't know that when we started out that cold November night.

The 'Possum Hunt
Written Autumn 1996

I could tell by his breathing that the old man, who was my grandfather, didn't have much longer to live. He was a few months short of ninety, and ready to let go of this life. My vigil at his bedside was more in the spirit of saying goodbye and wishing him bon voyage than it was grieving for him. He was finishing a long, good life and looking forward to the next great adventure.

We had been close while I was growing up, and once I had grown into a young man and my career took me all over the country, I always found time to come back to the remote farm to visit him. Sometimes I could spend only a few hours and sometimes a few days. We had sustained our close relationship through the years.

On my visits, he never failed to tease me about my first 'possum hunt. The old man loved to tease and loved to keep a joke going about someone or something. He'd wait until he had an audience and then say something like, "Winston, you were about seven or eight, somewhere about that on that cold November night you went wadin' in the creek weren't you?"

I'd laugh and say, "Yes sir, somewhere 'bout that."

Then he'd tell the story, and I think he enjoyed it more every time he told it.

Now, as I sat by the bed watching his breathing become more and more difficult, I remembered the strength and vigor that had been his on that long ago night of my first 'possum hunt. I was eight that year and he would have been about fifty-two—a tall broad shouldered, lean man, tempered by a life time of wresting a living from the hard red clay of that little farm in the foot hills of the Southern Appalachians.

I learned some things the night of that first 'possum hunt. One was that the old man wasn't going to take it easy on me just because I was only eight years old. If I was going to run with the big dogs, I had to act like one, and not like a puppy. It was a lesson I never forgot, one that helped me through a lot of rough situations as I clawed my way to the top of the corporate ladder in later years.

The old man had done more than any other person to influence the man I had become, and as I sat watching him die, I thought about that long ago November night.

It was a couple of weeks before Thanksgiving, the moon was rising full. I could tell it was going to be a good night for hunting. At twilight, the temperature had fallen into the low forties, and the old man had predicted that the night would bring the first hard freeze of the long Alabama autumn. A sure sign that winter was about to pounce.

I had been begging the old man to take me 'possum hunting since I could talk. His stock answer was, "Boy, you're not old enough, I'll let you know when. Now hush and let me have a little peace."

I didn't argue, it wasn't a good idea to argue with the old man once he said hush. But that didn't keep me from bringing the subject up from time to time. I didn't understand his reluctance to take me 'possum hunting. I was his constant companion in all the other activities around the farm. He had put a .22 rifle in my hand when I was six, and taught me how to sit quietly until I saw a squirrel in one of the tall trees down in the woods and shoot the squirrel out of the tree. He had given me a .410 gauge shotgun when I was seven and taught me how to lead the quick agile rabbit just enough to take his head off; but no matter how hard I begged I never got to go 'possum hunting.

Rabbit and squirrel hunting held no mystery for me, and I couldn't see much difference in these and 'possum hunting except that they were done in the daylight and 'possum hunting, due to the nocturnal nature of that little beast, was done at night. 'Possum hunting also seemed to have some kind of mysterious aura attached to it. Well, more than just that, there seemed to be a party atmosphere that went along with it. I can tell you I was smarting some because I had never been allowed to go along with the men on one of these hunts.

I had watched the men leave after supper and saw that their mood had certain exuberance about it. A mood that was missing from rabbit and squirrel hunting; and I had seen them return at dawn even more sprightly than when they had left the night before. I was puzzled for it seemed to my eight year old thinking that after a night of tramping the cold dark woods they should have been tired, and their steps should have been slow and dragging. Instead they would all be laughing and stepping sprightly, and even singing, as they brought the live 'possums home in the old tow sacks.

Late that afternoon I'd said, "Paw Paw, looks like it's gonna be a good night for a 'possum hunt." The old man just grunted and kept throwing hay to Red and Dan, the big red mules.

When we got up from the supper table later, the old man, without looking at me said, "If somebody wanted to go 'possum huntin' tonight, they'd be gettin' ready."

My heart jumped right up in my throat.

"They'd be callin' up the hounds, gettin' a sharp axe, puttin' kerosene in the lanterns, and gettin' a couple of tow sacks out of the barn."

It took me about twenty seconds to come panting back to the kitchen.

The old man looked at me, "Boy, what's ya hurry. The big 'possums don't walk 'til after midnight. Sit down over there in front of the fire and git warm, it's likely the last time you'll be warm this night."

About nine o'clock the old man went and got his heavy denim jacket and old felt hat out of the hall closet. I grabbed my old coat and a knit cap and followed him to the back porch were I had put the axe, tow sacks, and lanterns. The dogs were running up and down the steps, barking and begging, "Let's get going!" They were almost as anxious as I was.

As we passed the smoke house the old man said, "Hold on a minute boy, I got to git a little something outa here."

He disappeared into the dark building and I heard the sound of glass clinking against glass and then the sound of gurgling liquid, but I couldn't see what was going on in there. He came out of the smoke house and we started off across the cornfield, our breath coming in clouds of steam. I had to run to keep up as we crossed the big field, the old man was nearly a half foot over six feet tall and my eight year old legs had to work double-time to keep up with his long strides.

On the far side of the cornfield, dividing it from the woods, there was a creek. I hadn't thought much about it until we got there, but now I realized that we were a long way down the creek from the bridge, and I wondered how we were going to get across. We reached the creek and the old man waded right on through. It wasn't a deep creek the water only came to a little above his knees. I stopped at the edge of the cold swirling water and looked across at the old man on the other side.

"Well Boy, I thought you wanted to go 'possum hunting, if you do come on. If you don't, go on back to the house and curl up by the fire, your Maw Maw will most likely be glad to tuck you into a nice warm feather bed." I looked at the water glistening like ice in the moonlight and knew that if I failed this test I was a goner. I closed my eyes, sucked up my gut, and plunged in. The icy water came up to my chest, and it was swifter that it looked. I was almost to the other side when I stepped on a rock and slipped and fell, the undertow causing me to get a good ducking. By the time I struggled up the opposite creek bank all my clothes were soaked through, my hair was wet, and I was miserably cold. I've been in some cold places, spent January nights camped out on high mountains, but I've never been as cold as I was when I struggled out of that creek. I wanted to cry and run back to the house and the fire.

The old man looked at me standing there shaking from the cold, and said, "Might git nippy before the night's out, boy, you need to try to stay dry." With that he walked into the woods.

I followed him. It was darker in the woods and, if possible, even colder. We lit the lanterns and the glow seemed to help warm things up a little bit, maybe.

We scoured the woods looking for the illusive marsupial, the dogs running on ahead, me running with them, trying to keep warm, but we came up empty. Didn't see a 'possum, and I was getting colder and colder.

After a couple of hours, about midnight, I was about ready to tell the old man that I couldn't stand it any longer; I was so cold I was turning blue. About then, we walked out of the woods, on the side away from the house; it was the opposite side of the woods to the creek where we had entered. That put us as far away from the house as you could go and still be on the property. There had been a small cornfield here, and adjacent to it was a ribbon cane patch. The cane was ripe and ready for making syrup.

The old man stopped on the side of the cornfield by the ribbon cane patch, picked up some dead cornstalks, and piled them on the ground in the shape of a teepee. He dug a big wooden match out of his jacket pocket, struck it on the seat of his overalls, and lit the dry cornstalks.

"Boy, if you'll run over there to the woods and git us some dead sticks, we'll warm ourselves a little."

I jumped to it, I was cold as a well digger's rear-end and I was ready to get warm. There were actually icicles hanging off my britches legs. I got back with the firewood and we got a good fire going. I was turning round and round trying to warm all sides at once.

In a little while I was warm, and I walked over and cut a couple of stalks of purple ribbon cane. I came back to the fire and started to peel it and chew on its cold crispness, letting the sweet juice run down my throat. I looked over at the old man to offer him some of the cane, but he took a pint bottle of clear liquid from the bib pocket of his overalls, uncorked it, and tipped a generous portion of the liquid down his throat.

He didn't normally talk much, but that night he became more and more loquacious as the level of the clear liquid in the bottle kept getting lower. He told me stories about his life that night. He told me about things he had done and dreamed as a young man, about the victories and defeats of his life. Some of the things he had wanted and got and some of the things he had wanted and not got. It was a night to remember—one that I will treasure always. I knew that on this cold November night just before Thanksgiving when I was eight years old I had been initiated into manhood in the Tankersley family.

When the bottle was empty and the fire had died down, the old man threw some dirt over the last of the embers and once again the night was cold and dark, but now there was a difference, I was warm and dry and feeling pretty proud and satisfied with myself, I knew I'd passed the test.

As we re-lit the lanterns and started walking across the field in the opposite direction from which we had come, the old man said, "We better git going and find us a 'possum, else Grandma's gonna think we been sittin' out here by a fire with me drinkin' likker and tellin' stories. Step it up, I know where there's a big old persimmon tree, and 'possums just can't resist ripe persimmons."

On the way to the persimmon tree the dogs treed a young 'possum in a half grown yellow tulip poplar. After holding the lantern high to be sure it was a 'possum and not some other night animal, the old man took the axe and with powerful blows ringing in the still night air made short work of cutting down the tree. The tree fell and the young 'possum went into his only defense mode, pretending to be dead, *playing 'possum*, and the old man went over, picked him up by the tail, and dropped him in one of the tow sacks.

Before we got to the persimmon tree we could hear the dogs had already treed. They were jumping up as far as they could on the trunk of the tree and barking loud enough to raise the dead. One look told us that we had run up on a big old silver back 'possum. He was sitting up near the top of that big persimmon tree glaring at the dogs and us. He was a big and old, but he didn't look much like a gentleman.

The old man said, "Damned if I'm gonna cut down a good persimmon tree to get him. Boy, you're just gonna have to climb up there and shake him out."

I had a lot of trouble with that, that old fellow looked nearly as big as me, and he was a lot more at home in tree than I was. I didn't think I could do it. The old man looked at me with his "git on about it" look, and with shaking hands I grabbed the lowest limb and swung up in the tree. I passed the 'possum on the opposite side of the tree on my way up. He was snarling and snapping, but I was out of his reach. I got to the top of the tree and started shaking the tree with all my eight year old might. It took a while and I finally had to break off a limb and prod the 'possum, but the he finally went sailing out of the tree.

I had learned another valuable lesson: that I could do some things I thought I couldn't do, and I can tell you that's a lesson you need to know if you're going to get anywhere in life.

I flew down that persimmon tree and hit the cold ground about the same time old silver back did. He didn't even have time to play 'possum before I grabbed him by the tail and dropped him in the other tow sack, which the old man was holding open for me. I finally got the sack over my shoulder and with the old man bringing up the rear for once, we went toward home. I was struggling under the weight of the sack and the old man was staggering under the weight of the whiskey.

The old man stopped me a few hundred yards short of the house and said, "We don't ever talk to the women folk, especially your Grandma, about some of the aspects of 'possum huntin'". He could see that I knew what he meant and that he didn't have to explain any further.

And as we walked on through the cold night he was stepping right sprightly for an old fellow who had been out 'possum hunting all night. I think I even heard him singing a few words of *When You and I Were Young Maggie.*

I guess the last lesson I learned that night was you don't always have to tell all you know, especially to the women folk, and most especially to Maw Maw. That's a lesson I'm glad I learned at eight years old; I needed to know it when I was in some pretty intense negotiations at thirty-five.

I've thought about that night and its lessons many times in the intervening years, but it has never been as vivid as it was the night I sat and watched the old man, who had taught me so much to shape the man I had become, and whom I had loved for so many years, die.

I was a pall bearer when we buried him three days later. Some people, especially the old ladies who had always fussed at the old man about some of his habits; like drinking a little too much likker sometimes, chewing his home grown tobacco, not going to church, and cussing a little; might have thought I was disrespectful because I had a smile on my face as we lowered the coffin. But, I was thinking about all the fun the old man and I had when I was a boy and he was a man in his prime, and I was especially thinking about that long ago November night and my first 'possum hunt.

I just couldn't help but smile a little—hell, I'm surprised that I didn't laugh out loud—because I know the old man is out there somewhere, waiting to go on another 'possum hunt with me. Just as soon as I suck up my gut, wade that cold creek, and catch up with him again. This time though, my legs will be as long as his and we'll walk side by side, stride for stride.

Prelude to *Good Guys and Bad Guys; and Snakes and Bugs and Lizards*

I love to watch children playing in the garden. I'm sorry that I no longer have children around to play in Miss Beth's and my gardens. Sure they break a few plants, but that's easy to fix. The lessons they learn, however, may stay with them the rest of their lives. That's one of the points of the following essay.

Another point I make in this essay is that I believe insecticides aren't necessary to have a healthy ornamental garden. Don't you vegetable gardeners jump on me now I said ornamental! It is really difficult to grow vegetables in our part of the country without using insecticides. Quite the contrary, I believe that an insecticide-free ornamental garden will in a few years become a healthy garden—free of insects feeding on your prize plants. In this essay, I try to bring these two points together. That's the reason that my children and grandchildren were warned not to kill any animal or insect in the garden. Of course we let them catch a few lightning bugs on summer nights—one of the privileges of childhood. I sure wouldn't want them to grow up without that memory.

They didn't know the difference in the good guys and the bad guys, and that if they killed too many good guys, then the ecology of the garden would get out of whack, and we would have to wait a while for it to come back into balance. It takes a while for the good guys to get strong enough to take care of the bad guys.

The grandson mentioned in the story below is now grown and married, but I bet if you ask him about the good guys and the bad guys in the garden he will remember that it's okay to accidentally break a few plants while playing in the garden, but that it's against grandpa's rules to kill a living creature found in the gardens.

Good Guys and Bad Guys; and Snakes and Bugs and Lizards

Written Summer 1998

The garden, like life, is filled with good guys and bad guys. That is one of the most difficult things for most gardeners to accept. Gardeners are judge and jury when it comes to judging the good guys and the bad guys in their gardens. Unfortunately most gardeners, especially weekend gardeners, jump to the conclusion that all bugs and snakes are bad. Snakes, lizards and box turtles are often put to death without a trial. Toads stand a little better chance of surviving the gardener's wrath, but all too often these benevolent creatures are also hauled up before a *Judge Roy Bean* and executed. No insect stands a chance and therein is the tragedy of most gardens.

Not all the bugs and snakes found in the garden are villains. Our job as gardeners is to learn which bugs and snakes are good and which are bad. Box turtles, lizards, and frogs are good guys. They eat a lot of bugs.

I grew up in Alabama where we had rattlesnakes, cottonmouth moccasins and copperheads. I understand though that in the Upstate of South Carolina the copperhead is the only poisonous snake. The other snakes around here are non-poisonous, and non-poisonous snakes are the heroes of the garden. Poisonous snakes also feed on the same diet as non poisonous snakes, but for the safety of the children that play in the garden, the folks who visit the garden and the folks who work the garden they need to be relocated whenever possible and disposed of if this is not possible. All snakes eat a lot of voles and moles and other critters that love to feed on your prize plants, and snakes never attack plants and their roots as do some of the varmints they eat.

Many serious gardeners also place children in the category of garden pests. I'm a serious gardener and I not only allow, but I encourage, children to play in my gardens. I think it's a good place for them to learn that not everything people call bad is bad and that not everything that people call good is good. I also happen to think that gardens are for playing hide-and-seek, for hiding Easter eggs, and are good places for ten year olds to play Tarzan of the Apes and imagine that a lion is behind that big rhododendron around the next bend in the path.

I have five children. They're grown now, but when they were kids they played in my gardens. I have ten grandchildren who are almost grown; they also played in my gardens. I have three great-grandchildren. Unfortunately they live too far away to visit often enough to play in my gardens, but I hope there is a gardener near them that shares my philosophy.

I also encouraged my children and grandchildren to watch Tarzan movies, the old ones with Buster Crabbe and Johnny Weissmueller, not the new ones where the biggest adventure is when Tarzan and Jane jump in bed together. I want my grandchildren to watch the ones where Tarzan fights with crocodiles and lions—that's adventure. I encourage them to watch Batman and Superman movies: again, the Batman and Superman movies of the 1940s and 1950s, when their costumes were wrinkled and they portrayed good and evil as clearly as night and day. I don't encourage them to watch the ones of the 1980s and 1990s, where the costumes are perfect molded plastic and the lines between good and evil are so blurred that sometimes I can't tell the difference between the heroes and the villains. And, if Grandpa can't tell the difference, the kids *ain't* got a chance. I encourage them to watch Gene Autry and Roy Rogers movies. I'm glad the movie moguls haven't messed with Gene and Roy like they have Batman and Superman. I hope they never do. I know Gene and Roy wouldn't want to be modernized and believe if they were alive they wouldn't permit it. After all heroes should live on forever, even if it's just on celluloid.

I want my grandchildren to know the difference between the good guys and the bad guys in life and in the garden.

The only rule I make when they play in my gardens is don't kill anything that moves.

One day, a few years ago now, I overheard my six year old grandson telling his new friend, as they set off with home made bows and arrows to find them a lion in the back garden, "It's o.k. if ya break a bush or step on a flower, but don't kill no bugs or snakes or frogs, 'cause Grandpa's gonna get you if you mess with any of them. He says he can fix broke flowers, but he can't fix killed snakes and frogs and turtles and lizards and bugs".

Something that really concerns me about most of my gardening compatriots is that every time they see a plant leaf with a hole in it they grab the insecticide sprayer and spray everything in sight. Don't do it. It's bad for the garden, it's bad for you, and it's bad for the environment. If you spray insecticides indiscriminately you kill the good guys—I'm sure we've all noticed the sharp decline in the honey bee population in the last few years—along with the bad guys.

In the garden, as in life, if they are left alone the guys in the white hats will take care of the guys in the black hats, just like Gene and Roy took care of the guys in the black hats in those old western movies. But too many gardeners don't understand this process, they are afraid of snakes and think all bugs are bad, and they don't like lizards and frogs and box turtles much either. The secret of gardening success is to learn the difference between a ladybug and a bean beetle, they look a lot alike, but the ladybug is good and the bean beetle is bad. And learn the difference between a copperhead and a garden snake, which also look a lot alike, and both are good in that they eat a lot of the varmints that eat your plants—but you don't want to fool around with a copperhead.

I wish copperheads and Japanese beetles and white flies wore black hats, and garden snakes and ladybugs and praying mantises wore white hats. And I wish all the crooks in life wore black hats and the heroes all wore white hats like they did in those long ago Saturday matinee movies that brought magic to my life. It sure would make life and gardening easier.

Even better, it would make raising children easier.

Prelude to *Red-Tailed Hawks and Baby Chicks*

When Miss Beth and I first married in September of 1998 we knew we wanted to live on The Blessed Earth Farm. That left us with a big decision. We had to decide whether to live in the old farm house that was built in 1937 and was only about 1800 square feet or to build a new house down in the woods by the stream.

After a lot of thought and discussion we both decided that we had a third choice. We loved the old house, with its tongue-and-groove pine walls and ceilings, and its heart pine floors, too much to give it up. We decided to enlarge and modernize the house to fit our needs and to do it in such a way as to keep the feel of an old farm house. I'm happy to say we were reasonably successful in this endeavor. At least in our eyes we were successful. In the eyes of a decorator it might not appear that way, but that's what this new simple life is all about: looking at and doing things the way we want to, and letting the rest of the world go racing by on its own way—to where ever it's going.

Several months after we moved into the old farm house we still hadn't decided how we wanted to enlarge it. Then one afternoon one of the worst storms I remember came rolling in from the northwest. The dining room faces in that direction and, after about a half hour of the wind blowing the rain horizontally, I noticed that water was coming in around the big dining room windows.

This spelled big trouble, because I could reasonably extrapolate that water had been leaking around the windows for sometime and that the walls around the windows were most likely rotted.

Miss Beth and I had some discussion about it and decided that we should have the dining room wall knocked out and a glass room measuring fifteen feet by twenty-two feet built on to the house. There was also a carport at the opposite end of the house just off the master bedroom. We decided that we should have the carport enclosed with glass and add a gas fireplace to give us a nice little sitting room off our bedroom.

Out of all the good things we have done to the old farm house the best thing we did was to knock out the dining room wall and build the large glass room with clay tile floors. The room has a glass ceiling so all you see as you sit in the room is the glass, *cedar and clay tile of the room and then, of course, the great outdoors. This modern room joins the old dining room, with no wall or door in between. It's the modern butted against the old—but somehow it works.*

We named the room the garden room and it's where we spend much of our time. We can watch storms come and go and the seasons change, but one of the best things we watch is the big red-tailed hawk that hunts in the hayfield in front of the house. The field is about eighty acres, so the hawk has a big hunting ground.

RED-TAILED HAWKS AND BABY CHICKS
Written Summer 2002

Once upon a time, not many years ago, as amazing as it sounds today, baby chicks were more valued than big red-tailed hawks. That was the time when there were a lot of self-sustaining family farms and hawks were dreaded birds of prey. They swooped down out of the blue summer sky and made their dinner out of the baby chicks that roamed free with their mommas. The chicks were important, because farm families needed to raise them to adult fowl that would, if female, provide eggs for the breakfast table; if male, become fried chicken for the dinner table.

Any sighting of a hawk would bring the farmer running, shotgun loaded and more often than not the hawk became the prey and the baby chick lived to become chicken and dumplings.

In those once upon a time days, we didn't distinguish between the varieties of hawks. We called them all Chicken Hawks. We didn't think, or care, that they might do more good than harm. To us the immediate danger of losing a future meal, which we could ill-afford to lose was real, and the hawk was the villain sentenced to death without the benefit of trial, if you were good enough with a shotgun. My maternal grandfather, Mr. Willie Tankersley, was a master executioner. He rarely missed when he fired his big double barrel shotgun.

A big red-tailed hawk hunts the fields and pastures of The Blessed Earth Farm, I sit and watch him silhouetted against the high blue sky, soaring effortlessly, occasionally dipping a wing to correct his course, or flapping both wings once or twice to correct his altitude. But the pastoral scene is deceptive.

The moment the hawk sights some small mammal scurrying through the tall fescue grass of the field he transforms into a feathered missile. He tucks his wings tight against his body and plunges earthward. When it seems inevitable that he will crash into the ground the great bird unfurls his wings and unleashes his sharp talons to grab whatever small rodent he has targeted, then with great wings flapping he defies gravity and soars high above the ground.

If he has been successful in catching his prey he flies to the top of the dead oak tree on the north side of the field and sits atop the tall gray limbless column as he tears the small animal apart and devours it, his flashing amber eyes darting to all points of the compass guarding his dinner from poachers. When he has finished his dinner he rests on his lofty perch, surveying his kingdom. Sitting so still that he seems a part of the dead tree until it's time to hunt again.

One of the questions I'm most frequently asked by gardeners is, "How can I rid my garden of moles and voles?" I don't have a good answer for them. The little critters outwit us at every turn. We've devised poisons and traps with the ingenuity of a mad scientist. Still we go down in defeat. I have a good answer to the question, but not one that most people find acceptable. I tell them to go to the Spartanburg County Animal Shelter and adopt a couple of cats, and to be sure to have them spayed or neutered, feed them sparingly and turn them loose to hunt in the garden. Big red-tailed hawks would be better, but they're harder than cats to keep at home.

What I'm getting around to here is that if we gardeners are aware of the balance of nature in our gardens, then a lot of our problems will solve themselves. Most pests, especially insects and small mammals, such as voles and moles, get out of control because in our pursuit of perfection, at least our idea of perfection, we destroy their natural enemies.

Miss Beth detests snakes. When we married and she joined me at The Blessed Earth Farm, I had a full time job persuading her that the non-poisonous snakes I had encouraged to live in our gardens were there for a reason. They were there along with the cats to control the moles and the voles and the chipmunks and the rabbits and all the other small animals that loved to eat the roots and leaves of our beautiful ornamentals. I also had to convince her that we weren't committing animal cruelty when we fed the cats sparingly.

But most gardeners find benign snakes and even cats unacceptable in their gardens, and hawks aren't an option. So the small rodents prevail.

I never had any trouble with Miss Beth about the big red-tailed hawks. She likes to sit and watch them hunt as much as I do. I guess we've come full circle. Today we never see a baby chick following its momma around a farm yard, but we sure do admire big red-tailed hawks soaring high against the deep blue sky and if we got caught shooting one of the big birds, we'd most likely be arrested.

If Mr. Willie was still alive he'd be amazed that anyone would protect a hawk over a baby chick.

Prelude to *Prom Night was Moonlight and Roses*

I looked up from the menu and saw the young couple waiting to be seated. He was in a black tuxedo and she in a floor length gown. I could almost feel how nervous they were from across the room. It occurred to me that it was prom night for a lot of the high schools in the county. I called Miss Beth's attention to the young couple and whispered, "Prom night."

Memories of fifty-three years ago flooded through my mind. The year was 1950 and, for a moment, I could feel my own nervousness from that long ago time. I doubt that there is a time young men and women are as nervous as they are on prom night.

Times were different in 1950. We've made a lot of progress since then in most areas, except in music, and to me prom night and music go together. I can't imagine gliding across the floor with a girl in my arms to the music they have today. Maybe that's the point: they don't glide today they jump and twist and rant and rave.

That Friday night when we got home I couldn't get prom night 1950 off my mind so I wrote Prom Night was Moonlight and Roses.

PROM NIGHT WAS MOONLIGHT AND ROSES

Written Spring 2003

It's prom season: that magical, romantic time of year for high school juniors and seniors. Time for that first formal gown and for that first tuxedo, time for corsages and the first formal dinner date, a night for staying up until dawn, a time for falling in love and out of love, and for entering the world of being an adult tonight … but maybe going back to being a kid again tomorrow. Fifty-three years ago I took a lovely girl, who was later to become my wife, to my senior prom. We never fell out of love after that night. We were still in love when she died forty-seven years later.

I don't know much about proms today, but I know they are vastly different to the proms of 1950.

In 1950 the guys didn't have money for tuxedos; we wore whatever church clothes we had. I remember that I had a navy blue suit, bought on time using my daddy's credit, and that I paid two dollars a month on it until it was paid for a couple of years later. I wore the suit for my graduation ceremony, and that a few years later I wore it for my wedding.

Many of the girls didn't have money to buy gowns so they made their own. My gal made her gown. It was a pink, chiffon floating kind of fabric. Strapless was popular in those days. I was so innocent that I wondered how the dress defied gravity and stayed up.

I somehow found an extra dollar and a half, enough money to buy a corsage of gardenias, her favorite flower. I remember presenting the corsage to her in her momma's presence and trying to figure out how to pin it on her gown. There seemed to be a lot of flesh and not much fabric to work with. Finally her momma rescued me and took the corsage and pinned to the waist of the gown. I can still smell the fragrance of the corsage fifty-three years later.

We didn't go out to dinner before the prom. There was no money for such luxury and if we had had the money there was no place to go to dinner in our small town. We didn't rent a limousine, but went in my daddy's old 1940 Chevrolet that had 218,000 miles on it. It rattled and clanked, but it got us to the prom and home again.

We used the song *Moonlight and Roses* for the theme of our prom. The girls in our class spent days before the prom fashioning paper roses from colored crepe paper. The day of the prom the boys risked life and limb—at least that's what we told the girls—to climb ladders to hang the colorful paper roses from the rafters and walls of the gym. We were in no danger; we were just laying the groundwork for a good night kiss. Now fifty three years later I know the play acting wasn't needed the girls were just as anxious for that goodnight kiss as we were, but back then I didn't know that.

We had a small orchestra made up of the best of our marching band members. They probably weren't very good, but that night they were Glen Miller, Tommy Dorsey and Artie Shaw all rolled into one. We glided across the floor of the gym to the great old songs such as *Moonlight and Roses* and *Stardust* and *Polka Dots and Moonbeams,* and we ended with *I'll See You in My Dreams.* The chaperons looked the other way and the boys got to hold their dates especially close during this, the last dance of the evening.

The music has changed a lot since 1950, and the dances are different today. Today most boys have money to buy or rent a tuxedo, instead of wearing their Sunday suits; and the girls shop for weeks for just the right gowns and jewelry, instead of making their own gowns. Some guys rent limousines instead of driving their girls to the prom in an old clunker, and most couples go to restaurants for nice dinners before the prom, instead of nervously choking down a cheese sandwich.

But human nature hasn't changed. The circumstances, songs and customs of 1950 may sound quaint and even corny today. Our love songs may be a bit *smaltzy* for today's kids. But the kids will feel the same as we felt back then—nervous, excited, and romantic. Most of all, however, they will feel the magic of prom night ... the night of nights for high school juniors and seniors. Prom night is truly a rite of passage.

I still remember that good night kiss.

Prelude to *Life and Love is More than Wine and Roses*

I spent most of my adult life in the rough-and-tumble world of big business, but down deep I'm a romantic. I believe that my hard scrabble growing up and the demanding world of business taught me to recognize the difference in the worlds of romance and reality. I think that it takes a lot of tumbling around to wear off the sharp edges, and teach one the difference between the realism of Monday morning and the romance of Saturday night.

I confess here that my business travel and its demands upon my time kept me from being as romantic and spending as much time with my wife and children as I needed to and would have liked.

I love being a romantic on Saturday night, it's a lot of fun, but waking up on Monday morning and accepting the challenges of the real world is where we find lasting love and happiness. Monday mornings can be the most fun if we recognize that we can find love in changing dirty diapers.

I admit I didn't do most of the diaper changing. My wife and I tried to balance out the work load ... while I had five hungry mouths to feed; she had to do the feeding. We decided that her job was bigger than my job so, while she didn't hold down a job outside the house to bring in money, it was only fair that I pitch in after I got home in the evenings and before I went to work in the morning. We sorta went by the old, adage "A man's job is from sun to sun, but a woman's job is never done". I challenge all you young husbands and fathers to roll up your sleeves before and after work and on weekends, to help with the house work and the babies. That's how both you and your wife learn what love really is.

Too many people confuse romance with love. It's easy to believe that love is the candlelight and white linen table cloths of Saturday night, but that's romance. It's hard to remember that even though there's not much romance in Monday morning's crying babies, loads of laundry and dropping children off at school when we are already late for work, that Monday morning is where we find real love.

LIFE AND LOVE IS MORE THAN WINE AND ROSES

Written February 2002

Maybe there really is a little chubby guy with wings and a bow and arrow named Cupid and maybe he does cause people to fall in love, and live happily ever after, by nailing them with the love arrow he shoots from his bow.

Yeah, and maybe I can fly like that big red-tailed hawk that soars over the fields of The Blessed Earth Farm hunting for field mice, and maybe the world is flat, and maybe the moon really is made of green cheese.

I don't want to burst any bubbles about love, especially this close to Valentine's Day, but maybe we need a little plain talk about what real love is and what loving someone really means. Maybe if more people, especially our young people, could recognize that moonlight and roses and soft music and candlelight reflecting on white tablecloths is romance and not love we could save some marriages.

I'm all for romance. The world would be a poorer place without it. I like moonlight and roses and soft music and candlelight on white tablecloths, but that *ain't* what loving someone is all about. It's been a while since I glided across a dance floor to the strains of *I'll See You in my Dreams* with a beautiful young girl in my arms ... but I remember. It's been a while since I sat with my arms around a girl *counting all the stars and waiting for the dawn* ... but I remember.

Romance is Saturday night, sipping champagne and listening to soft music. Love is Saturday night sipping champagne and listening to soft music, but love is also Monday morning, waking up to reality when the Saturday night romance has long since faded. Love is scrimping at the end of the month to put food on the table when the paycheck has run out—and remembering the champagne. Love is long nights sitting up with sick babies and dragging to work the next day, and love is changing dirty diapers and stinking diaper pails. Love is long winter nights caring for sick children as streptococcus runs rampant through the family.

And, love is the simple pleasures.

Love is teaching your four-year old to ride a bike and kissing the wounds when the bike doesn't cooperate. It's teaching your two-year old to swim and giving him big hugs to sooth his fear of the water. Love is trips to the zoo and watching the awesome look on your child's face when she sees a polar bear for the first time.

Love is watching your young warriors come off the ball field and bursting the buttons off your shirt with pride whether the young warriors have their heads hung low in defeat or held high in victory. Love is watching your daughters come down the stairs for their first date with the young man who waits nervously for them by the bottom stair step, and your heart nearly bursts with pride at their beauty and budding womanhood.

Holding a grandchild in your arms—that's love; holding them all in your arms—that's really love. Worrying about your grown kids and their kids, wondering whether you've done all you can to prepare them for the things the world will throw at them—that's love.

Love is the dark lonely nights spent holding the hand of that pretty girl who, many years ago, glided across the dance floor with you to *Moonlight and Roses*, as cancer slowly takes her away from you and the awful helplessness you feel.

Love is picking up the pieces of your life and finding a new life. Love is the acceptance of your new wife into the family by your grown children, their spouses, and your grown grandchildren.

Love is giving just a little more when you have no more to give, and forgiving just one more time when the forgiveness cup is empty. Solving life's everyday problems, enduring the tragedies, and facing the future together with confidence—even when you're sometimes scared half to death—that's love.

Valentine's is a day of love and of romance. Enjoy the sweet verses of Valentine cards, and the special dinner with candlelight reflecting on the white tablecloth, and the wine and roses ... but remember, love is also everyday living. It's walking the high ridges and the lonesome valleys together.

Prelude to *"I Guess We'll Just Finish the Trip Together"*

In the fall of 1988, I decided to quit the demanding life of the busy business executive, and go and seek a different kind of life. One that I hoped would be more satisfying to me and my family.

I had worked hard for 37 years and had accumulated all the toys that successful, hard-working business executives consider essential. These toys didn't fit into my new life so I sold some of them and gave some of them away. For some reason, which I could never figure out, I kept a Cadillac that was about a year old at the time.

I kept it year after year until we were on the verge of growing old together—and I realized the old car and I had become attached to one another. Perhaps the following essay will give the reader an insight into the why. Maybe I'll even figure out why I held on to that old car. I sometimes find that if I don't know the why of something, writing about it will help me come up with the answer.

I Guess We'll Just Finish the Trip Together

Written Summer 2004

The elegant old Cadillac looks out of place sitting out there in front of the tractor shed beside the pickup truck, the big four-wheel-drive Bronco and the tractor. I never meant to keep that old car this long, but somehow 17 years have slipped by, and it's still a part of my life.

I remember the August afternoon in 1987 when I took delivery of the sparkling Brougham de Elegance Fleetwood Cadillac. The silver finish sparkled in the late afternoon sun. The big V-8 engine hummed quietly beneath the long hood that was clad with the distinguished Cadillac hood ornament, and there was room to spare for my long legs as I sat in the buttery leather seats.

The luxury car fit well with the life style I lived then as a busy business executive. When I left that life behind I divested myself of most of its trappings, but somehow I hung on to the Cadillac. I don't know why. I've viewed cars as transportation, as a way to get from one place to the other, since leaving the business life. During my business career I looked at automobiles not just as transportation, but also as status symbols. In the textile business, we preached so much against foreign imports, that we couldn't drive Mercedes and BMWs, which were becoming bigger status symbols than the big Lincolns and Cadillacs built in America. Now time has caught up with us, the old car and me, we've grown old together and that gives the car a special place in my life.

I now know that I'll probably never get rid of the Cadillac. We've become friends. It knows my moods and I know when it needs a little TLC. When I'm a little cranky and out of sorts the old car hums along almost as good as it did the day I drove it away from the dealer's showroom. When the old Cadillac is acting up and the big motor is missing, or drinking a little extra oil, I make allowances and don't push down too hard on the accelerator. After all time isn't a big priority to us now.

The old car died on me once and I killed it once, but the great mechanics at Barnett's Garage managed to revive it and make it go again. When the old Caddy died I had a factory-rebuilt motor put in to replace the one that was so addicted to motor oil that it drank itself to death.

A couple of years after that, I killed my old friend. I was on the way to an important appointment. I left home with time to spare and the old Caddy and I were just loafing along up Highway 221, when the red engine light came on. I thought the Caddy would be able to make it to my destination; it had never let me down before.

But a few miles further down the road steam gushed from under the hood. Still I drove on. Finally with a bang the heart of the old car gave up. I'd killed my old friend. I picked up my cell phone and called Mike Barnett at the garage and told him that I was leaving the victim of my crime beside the road and asked would he send a tow truck.

Later that day after I'd finished my business, business that really wasn't important enough to kill an old friend over, I called Mike and we held a consultation. I thought it was time to give the old Caddy a funeral befitting its dignified life, in a junkyard somewhere. Mike thought it was worth the considerable amount of money it would take to bring it back from the brink of the scrape heap. He agreed to fix the old Caddy at his expense and sell it and split the difference between the sale price and his cost with me.

About three weeks later I dropped by Barnett's Garage on Union Street, and the Caddy sat gleaming in the sun. I got in turned the key and the engine hummed like a new car. Mike was nice enough to let me out of our deal and I whipped out my credit card to settle the bill and called Miss Beth, my wife, to come drive my Bronco home. The Caddy and I took the long way home.

Once in awhile I clean up the old Caddy, take it out for a drive, put a little Frank Sinatra on the cassette player—no CD players for the old Cadillac—and think about when we both were new and shiny.

The old Cadillac and I have been a lot of miles and see a lot of life. I guess we'll just finish the trip together.

Prelude to *Miss Beth's Pasture Fence Garden*

Two years after I had my radical prostatectomy, my PSA started to rise again. After a radical prostatectomy a PSA reading of anything above zero is bad news. It usually means that the cancer is beginning to metastasize. As I said in the beginning we had decided to treat the cancer as aggressively as possible. My doctor determined that the strongest move we could make at this time was thirty-three radiation treatments to the area where the prostate gland had once been.

The treatments were to be given five days a week, with weekends off. We started the first of June and all was well until the middle of June. Then I began to sleep all the time. I could wake up to go to the bathroom, to bathe, and to eat, but that was about all I could stay awake for.

Miss Beth was taking care of our gardens. She had more energy than a team of big red mules and I admired the fact that instead of sitting in the house on those beautiful summer days she was willing to get out and do the things she wanted to do.

It's now September 11, 2007 and we are facing a much more serious situation with the cancer than we did in 1999. We know that the cancer has metastasized to the bones and that we are facing a terminal situation. We are almost through summer and it has been one of the most brutal summers on record. I have been confined to my recliner and the house most of the summer. Miss Beth has once again continued to do the things she likes to do outside, in spite of the summer breaking all heat records and it is close to breaking most of the drought records.

The gardens are prettier than ever. Not many people could have kept the gardens looking lush and healthy in the weather we've had.

MISS BETH'S PASTURE FENCE GARDEN

Written Autumn 2000

The lilacs are blooming in Miss Beth's Pasture Fence Garden. They're blooming right next to the sky blue iris. I have seen a lot of pretty things in my life, but the lilacs and the iris blooming together may be one of the prettiest. The blue of the iris is the perfect complement to the light lavender of the lilacs.

The story of Miss Beth's Pasture Fence Garden is also a beautiful thing. Most of the projects that happen on The Blessed Earth Farm are joint agreements between the two of us, but the Pasture Fence Garden is Miss Beth's. She dreamed it and she built it.

I missed most of the summer of 1999. Because of radiation treatments, I spent most of the summer in my recliner or in my bed reading and sleeping, and occasionally feeling well enough to do a little writing. I sometimes slept for several days at the time. It was during this time that Miss Beth dreamed her garden. She's not one to be content to dream her dreams as I sometimes am, so she executed her dream.

The pasture fence connects with the cathouse. (Cat house in this instance is where the cats of The Blessed Earth Farm sleep, not that other kind of cathouse. So please Mr. Sheriff, don't raid The Blessed Earth Farm.) The fence runs from the cathouse to the road, a distance of about two hundred feet, and has been overgrown with honeysuckle vines for as long as I have known the land that Beth and I now call home. In years gone by, I considered having a bulldozer come in and clear the vines and the fence. But then I would have had to build a new fence, and I do enjoy the fragrance of the honeysuckle. I also taught some of my grandchildren to suck the sweet nectar from the blooms when they were little shavers, and they enjoyed the nectar as much as they did candy and cake, so I forgot about the bulldozers and left the honeysuckle and the old fence it was climbing in place and in peace.

The big white bull also likes the honeysuckle. On hot summer days when the grass in the pasture is dry and brown, and I imagine not very appetizing even to a big white bull, he likes to lean against the fence and eat the leaves from the honeysuckle vines.

During one of my incapacitated weeks that summer, Miss Beth was walking along the fence and about fifty feet from the cathouse she spied a patch of winter jasmine that had been covered by the honeysuckle. On the spur of the moment she decided to clear the honeysuckle from around the winter jasmine, so that it could bloom its bright yellow blooms to cheer us in the deep of winter. By the time she stopped pulling honeysuckle vines, she had cleared the fifty feet of fence line from the jasmine to the cathouse. Miss Beth tore and ripped honeysuckle vines from the earth for two days as the hot summer sun blazed down. After wrenching the vines from the ground she realized that the soil from which she had pulled the vines was loose and rich from the many years of being deeply aerated by the roots of the big vines. The idea for her garden was born. The soil was so rich it didn't even need to be tilled it was already soft and friable.

There's still about one hundred-fifty feet of honeysuckle left from Miss Beth's Pasture Fence Garden to the road. So the big bull can enjoy the sweet taste of it and I can enjoy the sweet smell of it.

Miss Beth then decided that the area she had cleared would be a perfect location for some of the plants she had dug, put in pots, and brought with her from her garden in Converse Heights when we married, and she joined me at The Blessed Earth Farm, especially her lilacs and her hostas. Before she could stop herself she had planted a garden about ten feet wide and fifty feet long. She planted great mounds of pink, purple, and white thrift near the sunny border by the lawn, woodland poppies in the shade of the great old crape myrtle that was there already, fragrant glossy leaf gardenias, rabbit-eye blueberry bushes, great southern hollyhocks, autumn joy sedum, and many other plants. She planted and planted until the garden was full.

Then she sat back, looked at her garden, and decided it needed a border. She hauled rocks from the barn lot, a distance of two football fields, in a garden cart, pulling the heavy rock laden cart uphill for days. (I could have hitched the trailer to the big Ford Bronco, filled the trailer with rocks and pulled them up the hill in one load, but I was sick and when Miss Beth decides she wants something done she wants it done right then.) She lifted the rocks out of the cart one by one and lovingly laid them to her liking until she had bordered the front and ends of the garden with the rocks. Her Herculean labor had won her. The pasture fence formed the back border of her garden.

Miss Beth had her garden and I still had about one hundred and fifty feet of honeysuckle-covered fence. We were both surprised the next time the big white bull leaned against the fence near the new garden for his delicacy of honeysuckle leaves, and the fence along the garden fell down. It was old and rusted and the wooden posts were rotted. The honeysuckle had been holding the fence up, and not the other way around the way around. But it doesn't cost much to build a new pasture fence and while we were at it we put in a new gate so we could go around back and see Miss Beth's Pasture Fence Garden from the other side. After all a new garden, especially one built with such an abundance of love and labor deserves a new fence.

A lot of good things in life can come by taking advantage of a bad situation. Miss Beth could have sat by my side, while I slept and felt sorry for both of us being confined while I was fighting the cancer that was lurking within my body, but she elected to do something. She built something beautiful instead feeling self pity. It's surprising what beautiful and good things can happen to us when we just start something ... instead of feeling sorry for ourselves.

The garden is beautiful this year. I've just walked outside in the rain and stood looking at it. It satisfies my soul that something so good came out of one of the lowest times of my life. I have thanked Miss Beth many times for the garden, it's one of our smallest gardens, but it really warms our hearts when we think of the summer Miss Beth spent building it.

Thank you for the garden Miss Beth, but thank you mostly for a great lesson about living through tough times.

Prelude to *Maggie, Big Boy and Tabby*

I asked Elizabeth Sabin to marry me in July of 1998. She said yes, and we started planning the wedding to take place as soon as possible. At our age it doesn't pay to put things off.

Elizabeth Anita Sabin, who shall be known as Miss Beth from here forward, was a city gal and I lived on a farm, but she was agreeable to selling her house in town and joining me on The Blessed Earth Farm. She wanted to take a shot at being a country gal, and it turned out she's a natural for the rural life. Life on The Blessed Earth Farm has become so natural for us that neither of us can imagine ever living in the city again.

We really had only one problem to solve about her moving to the farm. Miss Beth had a beautiful sixteen year old cat named Maggie that she loved very much. Maggie was an indoor cat and she was the ruling queen of Miss Beth's home. She also had a big one-eyed Tom cat named Big Boy. Big Boy came in and out of the house as he pleased. Miss Beth loved having the animals around her in the house in the evening.

I had been raised on a working farm where the philosophy that animals were outdoor creatures that earned their keep had been instilled in me as a youngster and I had never learned to think of animals as pets ... just to love and take pleasure having as companions, the way Miss Beth had.

I felt so strongly about this that Miss Beth agreed that she would find homes for Maggie and Big Boy instead of bringing them to the farm with her, since I was against having animals in the house, and with all the 'coons, foxes, coyotes and other nocturnal animals that roamed the farm the two cats wouldn't have lasted through the first night outside.

One night a few weeks before Miss Beth and I were going to be married I went over to her house for supper. After supper Miss Beth was sitting in a recliner. Maggie climbed up on the back of the chair put her front legs around Miss Beth's neck as though her legs were arms and started to nuzzle on Miss Beth's neck. Suddenly, I realized how selfish I had been, because of the things I had been taught in my early life about animals, I came very near making the mistake of letting Miss Beth make a sacrifice which would have made both our lives poorer.

Mr. Willie, my maternal grandfather, wasn't wrong in what he taught me, it was just that we now live in a different time, and I hadn't changed with the times. And we certainly had enough that we didn't need to worry about sharing with two cats. These cats didn't need to earn their keep. I told Miss Beth that if she loved me enough to give up Maggie and Big Boy, two animals she dearly loved and that had been with her much longer than I, and she was giving them up without a mummer of complaint, then I certainly loved her enough to learn to live in the same house as Maggie and Big Boy. Thus, Maggie and Big Boy moved to The Blessed Earth Farm and all our lives became more blessed.

I have never regretted this decision. In fact, it is one of the best things that happened to me. I learned to love animals as pets, adding much pleasure to my life. Maggie and Big Boy are both dead now. I took their deaths as hard as Miss Beth. Maggie's death was especially hard for both of us, for she had become the queen of The Blessed Earth Farm, and reigned with dignity and pride.

MAGGIE, BIG BOY AND TABBY

Written Summer 1998

I did a lot of my growing up on the hardscrabble farm of my maternal grandfather, Mr. Willie Tankersley, in the east-central foothills of the Appalachian mountains of Alabama. Mr. Willie was tough—he had to be to wrench a living out of eighty-eight acres of red clay. One of the things Mr. Willie taught me was that people and animals had to earn their keep or they had to be kindly and expeditiously dispatched. People who didn't earn their keep were asked to leave—family or not. When animals didn't earn their keep, Mr. Willie took his twelve-gauge off the wall and a shovel from the barn. He then walked the animal to the woods. Mr. Willie, the shotgun, and the shovel came back. There just were not enough resources in that life to support people or animals that didn't carry their load—times were hard.

I have always embraced the philosophy Mr. Willie taught me that animals as well as people must earn their keep … or at least I did until I met Miss Beth, Maggie, and Big Boy and came to love them all. They taught me a lesson that has added a lot of pleasure to my life. They taught me that animals, especially cats, can earn their keep just being pets.

In addition to Pepper, the big German shepherd that romps through the pasture and woods of The Blessed Earth Farm with us, and the cows and calves and the big white bull, we have three cats that live on The Blessed Earth Farm. I think cats, just like children and dogs belong in the garden. Dogs and children sometimes break things in the garden with their rambunctious play. Cats are gentle. I don't think I've ever seen one break a plant. They like to nibble on leaves of the plants sometimes, but that's the most *damage* I've ever seen a cat do in the garden.

Maggie, Big Boy, and Tabby are all domestic felines, but that's about all they have in common. Maggie is the reigning queen, Big Boy is the strutting, aging prince, and Tabby—well Tabby is the unobtrusive worker of the group.

Maggie and Big Boy are immigrants. Miss Beth brought them with her when we married and she came from the city to live at the farm. Tabby is a native. My daughter, Emily, brought Tabby's great-grandmother to the farm to live about ten years ago. Tabby was born on the farm and so far as I know has never been outside its boundaries except for a visit to the vet, to eliminate any future reproduction occurrences, when she was about four months old.

Maggie is a house cat, but she, true to her queenly nature, commands Miss Beth to take her out to the front garden for about fifteen minutes each day. Maggie walks along slowly and regally, like the old monarch she is, cocking her head occasionally to look and listen.

Miss Beth follows slowly behind her like the handmaiden Maggie considers her to be.

Maggie's goal is always the same; a clump of tall fescue grass that grows in an otherwise neat garden of blue salvia, gray lamb's ear, pineapple sage, sprawling purple verbena, and fragrant viburnum. Visitors often ask me why that one clump of tall fescue is left to prosper in the otherwise grass free garden. I think I'm going to have to put up a sign that reads "Maggie's Grass". When Miss Beth obeys Maggie's charge to take her outside, the clump of fescue is always her destination. She approaches her grass on tiptoes, daintily munches a few sprigs, then turns to Miss Beth and as though to say, "You may take me back inside now, I've finished in the garden for today and it's time for my nap".

When the fescue grows too tall and tough to suit Maggie's taste, Miss Beth takes her scissors and cuts it down by about half, so that new tender shoots can grow back for Maggie to chew on each day. Like the Regal she is Maggie refuses to go out on days when it's rainy and windy. Maggie sleeps in the bed with us. She wants to sleep in the middle, but Miss Beth is firm about that, she makes Maggie sleep on the side of the bed.

Big Boy, the aging prince, struts around like he owns the farm and everything else in sight. I'm pretty sure he thinks he does. Big Boy has only one eye. He lost his left eye in a contest with an automobile before he was old enough to learn that there are some things even he can't conquer. But he sees all he needs to see out of his one eye. Big Boy comes in and goes out of the house as he pleases and he roams the land at will. I see him walking the trees that have fallen across the creek strutting as though the trees were felled just for him to use as footbridges. He hunts in the underbrush that grows along the creek and swaggers proudly through the perennials and woody ornamentals like they were planted just for his pleasure. I believe he thinks that we propagate, plant, and tend the gardens for his pleasure. He lurks stealthily under the many bird feeders Miss Beth has placed around the gardens. It saddens us when he is successful in one of his sneaky pounces and catches a bird, but we write it off to the laws of nature.

Tabby is a sleek, stealthy, competent outdoors cat. She loves barns, but shuns houses and people with a passion. Miss Beth feeds her once a day. She treks down to the barn just as it's getting light enough to see and places Tabby's food on the roof of the low shed that covers the cattle-loading chute on the north side of the barn. Tabby usually comes to eat and allows Miss Beth to love her a little. That's about the only time we see Tabby and the only time anyone touches her—that's the way she wants it. Once in a while when we're working the shade garden next to the stream we'll catch a glimpse of a furry orange ball as it flashes by chasing a vole or a mole or whatever small creature Tabby is stalking that day. Tabby earns her keep.

I'm sure glad Miss Beth and Maggie and Big Boy taught me to love animals—especially cats.

Prelude to *Pepper*

Most folks learn the lesson that not everything works out the way they want it to at an early age. The following essay is an example of something that started so right, with such good intentions, but turned out about as bad as it could. It's a perfect example of the saying that nobody ever said life was going to be fair.

Not long after we married, Miss Beth and I decided that we needed a dog to go with all the cats at The Blessed Earth Farm. I once had a German shepherd named Pepper. Pepper was the best dog I ever had so Miss Beth and I decided we would get another German shepherd puppy and name it Pepper, II. Of course, the II was dropped from the name before we got Pepper home from the breeder's kennels. All my, now grown children, had played with Pepper I when they were children. They sat on her, pulled her tail, and did about all the things kids do when they're playing with dogs ... and Pepper never objected. There was never a growl or a bark or a deep rumbling in her chest.

The story of the new Pepper turned out very differently. Later you will read about the two little rascals. Maybe there's a lesson here, when you compare the story of Pepper and the two little rascals that dogs like people don't always have to have papers showing that they are pure bred. Sometimes the mutts turn out better. Pepper was a blue blood: the little rascals were of very uncertain lineage.

PEPPER

Written Spring 1999

It's a secluded and beautiful place, the ravine that is carved by the stream that runs from the big spring below the barn on The Blessed Earth Farm. It was Pepper's place—the place she could roam and romp, free of fences and leashes. Miss Beth and I may hold the deeds, but for as long as she lived that particular part of the property belonged to the big German shepherd. She made it hers through her joy and wonderment in it.

Miss Beth and I brought Pepper to The Blessed Earth Farm when she was a tiny ball of fur all black, sans a few tan markings, and big round eyes the color of coal in a dark, sooty cellar. She grew well here on the farm. She grew into a beautiful eighty-pound package of bone and muscle. But she had a flaw—she grew up to be anti-social.

Maybe we took her from her momma and her brothers and sisters too early, but the breeder said it was time. Or maybe I didn't check out the breeder's reputation as well as I should have, or maybe he needed the money that day when he urged us to take the puppy at six weeks old. We wanted to wait until Pepper was twelve weeks old to take her from her momma and her siblings, but the breeder insisted that it was okay at six weeks. Maybe it was growing up on the farm with just Miss Beth and me and the other creatures that roam the farm for company. I just don't know.

We tried to socialize her. We tried to take her places where she would be in contact with other dogs and other people. We took her to town about once a week and to PetSmart when we went to buy dog and cat food and other animal supplies. She seemed to enjoy touching noses and smelling around the other dogs as dogs are inclined to do. But as time went on, she began to growl and then bark at the other dogs and finally she would try to attack the other dogs so we had to stop taking her when we went into town to get supplies.

She grew up to love Miss Beth and me, and I think she even liked the cats, though she didn't show it. I'm pretty sure she liked the cows and though she made a sport of chasing them she never showed any animosity toward them. Sometimes she just ignored them—even the big white bull, and he's hard to ignore—and went about her business of roaming the woods and playing in the stream.

Around Miss Beth and me she was always like a puppy—full of loving playfulness and eager to please; but, she was beginning to show a definite dislike for people and other animals especially other dogs. Our veterinarian, Dr. Ed Davidson, a good friend, tried to help us with her behavior problems, but he warned us that she would probably not change.

As Pepper grew bigger and stronger it became obvious that we had to find a different place for her, a place which had people more adept than us in handling the big German shepherd's aggression. But then we had to take her out of obedience school for trying to bite all the people, and fight with all the dogs. And except for her walks in the pasture, down along her beloved creek, we had to keep her in her run or on leash.

She was still a young dog, but we were beginning to realize that she was becoming a danger. We just didn't realize how much of a danger she could be: there was never a better case where the old adage "love is blind" applied, than it did in ours with Pepper. We loved Pepper too much to see the problem clearly.

Our vet had hinted that putting her to sleep might be the only solution to the problem. I wish our vet had been a bit more direct about the necessity of putting her to sleep. Our hearts were so much in the problem that our brains couldn't see the answer clearly. We enjoyed our walks with her. Everyday walking with Pepper was a new experience.

There was the day when we came upon the great blue heron fishing in a still, deep pool along Pepper's creek. She watched the great blue rise into the air and settle to fish again, just out of sight around the bend. But there would be no fishing for the great bird in Pepper's creek that day. The game was on. Pepper rushed after the bird, barking in her deep terrifying tone. The outcome was predetermined. The big blue bird spread its great wings and soared away from Pepper, and all earth-bound creatures, to fish another creek or pond or pool that was friendlier to big blue birds.

I can remember her as she smelled a rue anemone in spring, or dug at a yellow dandelion. I remember how I watched her, a gangly half grown dog, chasing the grasshoppers that flew up out of the tall fescue of the pasture in the summer time. And I saw again, the puzzlement on her face when she caught one of the grasshoppers looking at me as though saying 'what do I do with this thing, whatever it is.' I visited again the amazement reflected in her now brown, almost bourbon whiskey colored, eyes when she saw her first rabbit. I don't know which was more startled Pepper or the rabbit as she chased it out of the pasture and into the woods beyond.

But most of all I remembered her powerful, ground eating lope as she ran free with an effortless gait across the hills and ravines of the pasture and woods; muscles bunching powerfully in her haunches and legs.

I wasn't going to be up front near the road but a minute that day when I let her out of her run without putting her on leash, but it turned out that a minute was too long. She'd never done it before, but I saw her bunch up her muscles as the pickup truck came down the road. I wasn't far from her, only a few feet, but I couldn't reach her in time and she ignored my voice command to *come* and then to *stay*. She attacked the truck head on. I guess she thought that like the cows it would turn and run.

The man stopped his truck and came back to the motionless dog and me. He simply said, "I'm sorry." I knew he could see my hurt and was trying to help. I told him that he couldn't help it, and he got in his truck and went on down the road.

I've relived the scene hundreds of times in my mind, and each time I do I realize how lucky I was that it was a pickup truck coming down the road at forty miles-an-hour instead of a child on a bicycle coming down the road. We lost a dog that we had come to love, but it may have been one of the luckiest days of our lives.

I got Miss Beth from the house and we went down to Pepper's favorite spot by the creek and dug an almost man size grave in the hard dry summer dirt. We wrapped her body in a shroud fashioned from one the cloths which I used to tote leaves in the fall time of the year—one of the ones she used to grab with her teeth, adding to my already heavy load of leaves. When we finished we picked big smooth rocks out of the creek bed and covered the grave. Miss Beth was sure that each rock was placed to her liking.

Somewhere the big dog runs free, her powerful haunches and legs carrying her effortless through greener pastures and along clearer streams than she has ever before known.

Prelude to *A Mother's Day Rose*

We often buy something and find that we received less than we paid for. But once in a while, we have the very pleasant surprise of getting more than we knew we were buying. This is the story of just such an experience.

I carefully walked the land, inspected the house and out buildings and had the land surveyed, so that I could check the boundaries, before I bought the farm in the spring of 1990. I still missed, however, one of the most valuable things that was included in the package. The seller didn't know that it was valuable either, nor did it matter to her when she found out it was valuable to me, because the value was sentimental. This is the story of one of those serendipity happenings that can make life so pleasing.

A MOTHER'S DAY ROSE

Written Spring 1998

It's Mother's Day and the rose is blooming.

I'm a great-grandfather and I still think about my momma, Mary Alice Tankersley Hardegree, almost everyday. But on Mother's Day when I think about momma and the rose, I cry a little. I don't let people see me cry, it's a private time and the generation to which I belong declares that daddies, granddaddies, and great-granddaddies don't cry ... but they do.

I still have a little trouble getting used to the fact that in today's world men are allowed to cry. I guess crying is good for men, as it is for women and children; I have found that it helps my feelings. It's just that I'm from a generation that thought men shouldn't cry. But, on Mother's Day, when I bring out some of the precious memories of my childhood, and think about how much my momma loved me and about all the sacrifices she made for me I still cry, but I keep it private. Momma wouldn't have wanted me to cry where other people could see. She was raised even harder than I was.

In that long ago time, when I was a boy, it was a custom for people to wear a rose on Mother's Day. A red rose told people that your mother was alive. A white rose signified that she was dead. I don't know if this custom is still around or if it is one of the lovely mores that has been lost in the twilight zone of hand held computers and wireless living.

The rose was red and I remember how proud I was to wear a bud from it on Mother's Day. I was lucky, I had my momma, but I still remember how sorry I felt for those kids who wore a white rose on Mother's Day. Early on the Sunday morning in May that was Mother's Day, as soon as I was dressed, I would go to the east side of the house. On the east side of the house the rose captured the gentle morning sun and it grew well there. With momma's scissors I would snip off a big red bud and run in the house to get momma to help me pin it on ... I never was much of a hand with pins. I would proudly wear my rose bud all day, and by dark it would be wilted and the petals would be falling off. When I walked to the bedroom to get undressed on Mother's Day night it looked like I was leaving a trail of blood.

I don't know the name of the rose. I never did, and I haven't been able to find it in any books on roses, and I've consulted a bunch of them. I've had several rose experts come out to the farm, but none of them know the rose either. I lost the rose for fifty years. But I found it again. It was the extra value surprise in the package when I bought the farm.

When I bought the old house and the land that I later named The Blessed Earth Farm about ten years ago, I thought I was buying a place to spend my weekends, and a few days each week raising vegetables and propagating woody ornamentals. But as the years passed I fell in love with the old house and the land, and after my first wife, Martha, died I decided to live there. I didn't know when I wrote the check and took possession of the little farm that I was buying a place to build the most precious memories of my life.

I also didn't know that I was buying a long lost precious memory of my childhood. I didn't know I was buying two of the old red roses of the Mother's Days of my boyhood. They were growing in the front yard. They were part of the deal. I closed on the property in March. As I worked to adapt the property to my needs, I noticed the two big rose bushes growing out front, but I didn't pay much attention to them. In May, about a week before Mother's Day, the buds started to show color and in a few days the buds had opened enough that I could tell I had found the same old rose of which I so proudly snipped a bud to wear on Mother's Day, when I was a boy.

The lady who sold me the farm, Sue Rogers, was still living then, and lived just up the road. I walked the half mile or so, up to her house, to ask her about the history of the rose and if she knew the name of it. She told me that a friend had given her the two rose bushes when they were about a foot tall. She had planted the two roses soon after she and her husband had built the house in 1937. But, she didn't know the name of the rose either. The rose had grown and prospered all those years without any care, except for a little extra water once in a while, when Miss Sue happened to think about it.

Since I've owned The Blessed Earth Farm, I've propagated dozens of young plants from the old rose bushes. I've given them to friends and strangers ... to anyone who happened to notice them and want one. I gave a whole truckload to some of my friends who own houses in the Habitat for Humanity neighborhoods in Spartanburg. And, I've planted several more in the gardens of The Blessed Earth Farm.

It's Mother's Day, and again the rose is covered with blood red blooms and buds. Today I'll be wearing one of the buds from the rose to honor my momma. I probably should wear a bud from a white rose bush, but I don't know whether the old custom still reigns: besides my momma is still living in my heart, and always will be. So, I believe this justifies wearing the red rose bud. (I've found that I can rationalize almost anything if I put my mind to it.)

Since I've never been able to find the name of the rose I'm gonna name it the Red Rose Of Mother's Day.

Prelude to *A Red Rose and a Hug and Father's Day*

My father, David Archibald Hardegree, was one of the kindest, gentlest men to ever live. He died in 1951 when he was forty-one, and I was nineteen.

I've had a blessed life, but even blessed lives have regrets. One of the greatest regrets of my life is that my father died so young, and I was deprived of his love and guidance once I became a man, and set out to raise my own family and build my own career. There were many times when I needed an older man in my life that I could trust: I needed a daddy with whom I could just sit and talk, and ask for advice and guidance, man-to-man.

I also regret that he never knew his grandchildren, and they never knew him. They would each have been proud and pleased with one another.

He did leave me with many memories of what life is like when you are gentle, kind, and loving. I couldn't have had a better role model for kindness and gentleness. He also left me many goals to reach if I were to measure up to him in kind and gentle and loving ways of life. I don't think I've made it, but Dad, I've tried.

We lived in an age when men and boys didn't hug or show affection or say I love you to one another. I wish I could have my daddy back to hug once more and to tell him I love him. Of all the men of his generation that I have known, I believe that he would understand men hugging. He would also understand that it's okay for men to cry.

He would understand me wanting to wear a red rosebud on my lapel on Father's Day to honor him.

A Red Rose and a Hug for Father's Day
Written early Summer 1994

I had a wonderful daddy, and I loved him a lot, but I never hugged him and told him that I loved him—at least not after I was six or seven years old. He deserved roses and a hug from me on Father's Day—and every other day of the year. But in my generation of the 1940s, daddies didn't get flowers or hugs from their sons—they fought wars. (Actually, my generation was born in the 1930s, but having been born in 1932, the 40s are really the years I remember as my growing-up years. So, I relate the basic mores and customs of my life more to the decade of the 1940s.)

In my generation daddies and sons didn't hug; and sons didn't wear roses to honor their daddies on Father's Day it would have been considered *unmanly*. Daddies were only honored with flowers at their funerals, never with red and white roses on Father's Day, as mothers were on Mother's Day.

I didn't have my daddy long, since he died so young—but I have my memories of him. He loved gardening, and I believe that my same love of gardening was inherited from him.

I have only a few pictures of him. One of the pictures I have of him was made around 1944, and shows him climbing out of his old 1940 four-door Chevrolet sedan—he drove that car two hundred and eighteen thousand miles. He and that old black Chevrolet were practically inseparable. The automobile companies didn't make cars from 1942 to 1946. These were the years of World War II, when they were too busy building tanks and other vehicles of war.

In the picture Dad is all dressed up in a suit and tie and hat. A man wore hats and suits and ties a lot in those days. Dressing up differentiated the white-collar from the blue-collar worker and white-collar workers dressed up even when they were just going to visit a relative. In my favorite picture of dad, his hat is set at a jaunty angle and he has a *happy-go-lucky* grin on his face.

Miss Beth surprised me with framed enlargements of the few pictures I had of my daddy and momma a few years ago. She didn't do it for a special occasion; she just did it because she's the kind of thoughtful person who thinks about those things, and she has the resilience to act on them after she thinks of them.)

Momma had more pictures of him, but after she died I let my brother and sister have them. The few pictures I kept of him were more to my liking than all the rest—it showed him the way I remembered him. He was a man's man, but he had a heart of gold, and a *devil-take-the-hindmost* attitude toward life.

I envy my children's generation—they were born in the 1950s and 60s—their children, both sons and daughters, have been hugged by their daddies all their lives, but the best part is that the daddies get hugged back. My sons taught me that it was okay to hug them after they were grown. I didn't hug them much when they were growing up—it wasn't *cool*. But I sure enjoy the hugs today.

No matter what your age it is okay to hug your daddy and tell him that you love him. And Daddies, even if you belong to my generation or the generation before mine that fought the *big war,* it's okay to hug your sons. You can tell them you love them too: it *ain't* sissy. I guarantee you're both going to like it and have good memories about it for as long as you live.

Oh, and yes, it's okay to wear a rose for your daddy on Father's Day. The Mother's Day rose is still blooming. It's red, but I'm going to wear one today even though my daddy has been dead a half-century—he's still living in my heart. I wish he was here so I could hug him, and tell him how much I love him and how much I appreciate all he did for me.

Prelude to *Bob Edge, Rhododendrons and Sausage Biscuits*

I mention serendipity several times in these essays. I don't think anyone can know when or how a serendipity moment will happen. We can define the word, that's not the problem. But, the actual serendipity occurrence is a magical thing and not truly comprehensible until it has happened. We never know when it's going to happen or how it's going to happen. I do know that in my life those serendipity moments have usually happened at times when I was in need of something good and unexpected to happen.

Some of us seem to have more serendipity moments than others do. I seem to be blessed with such moments especially since 1988 when I quit the busy business executive business and turned to the pursuit of a more simple life. I think this is because since that time I've been more willing to forego detailed plans. Now I'm content with just seeing what the day brings, rather than trying to make the day bring what I think it should.

Meeting Bob Edge was one of those serendipity days. I must have eaten hundreds of sausage biscuits, "with a little mustard please," in Hardees' restaurants over the years, but Bob Edge is the only person I ever saw, in all those hundreds of days of eating sausage biscuits, that I wanted to introduce myself to. "I was a stranger in a strange land" and in need of a friend. A serendipity morning brought me that friend.

BOB EDGE, RHODODENDRON AND SAUSAGE BISCUITS
Written Spring 1990

The rhododendrons are in bloom, and each morning I walk in the garden admiring the big bright trusses of blooms.

As I walk I name each of the cultivars to myself—*Roseums Elegans, English Roseum, Catawbanese Alba, Cynthia, Anna Rose Whitney* and on through the eight varieties growing in my garden. And, as I walk I think about my good friend, Bob Edge. I'm sure Bob is walking with me and correcting me when I make a mistake.

It was Bob who taught me about rhododendrons. He was the first friend I made when I moved to Spartanburg. We met because of our mutual addiction to Hardees's sausage biscuits and our friendship developed through our mutual interest of horticulture and gardening.

Bob had a little nursery in back of his house on Oak Grove Road where he propagated rhododendrons from stem cuttings, and we used to spend hours there in the shade of the big pine trees as the master taught the eager student. Bob was so well known for growing quality rhododendrons that each year's crop would sell out in a matter of days, and often Bob would start a waiting list for the following year.

Early in our friendship Bob told me that he was being treated for prostate cancer. As our friendship grew Bob would keep me posted on how the cancer was invading his body. As his health worsened, we intensified our learning sessions. Finally one May morning, over a sausage biscuit, he told me that we needed to take some cuttings and begin sticking that year's crop. We usually did this in July, so I told him I thought we were pushing the season a little. He said that he was aware of that, but that he thought we needed to start early this year. I now know how Bob felt as I face exactly the same situation: prostate cancer that has metastasized to the bones. You don't know exactly when, but you know that death is near by.

We took 4,000 cuttings from the stock plants at his nursery that year, and brought them out to The Blessed Earth Farm to stick. I was looking at my old diaries just the other day, and I still have our crop from that year listed by the number of cuttings and the cultivars. Bob didn't feel well enough to help much, but he sat by the potting table, correcting my mistakes, as I filled the pots and stuck the little cuttings to root. Bob died in July of that year. I'm glad that we listened to his premonition to start early. He lived to see the plants take root.

The success rate of rooted cuttings in that crop was the best I've ever had. About 85 percent took root and about 70 percent of the cuttings that rooted grew into healthy young plants. I didn't sell any of these plants. It seemed as though it would be almost sacrilegious to sell the last crop of rhododendrons that Bob and I did together. I decided they would be Bob's legacy to his friends. I planted some and I gave some to Bob's friends, and some to my friends. I gave some to the Spartanburg Men's Garden Club for their annual plant sale, and I gave the last batch of about one hundred plants to my good friend, the late Dr. Sam Black, to plant in the woods surrounding his house. Sam loved rhododendron about as much as Bob and I did. I propagated many crops of rhododendrons after Bob's last crop, but none were as successful as our last one together.

Bob and I propagated thirty-three cultivars of rhododendrons that last year, all of which Bob had growing in his garden as stock plants for his nursery. In the years since then I have picked eight of these cultivars, which grow best for me in the soil and climate of the Upstate of South Carolina.

Rhododendrons can be difficult to grow in the heavy clay soils and the hot humid weather here in Spartanburg. The secret is in the way they are planted and in the cultivars selected.

To plant, dig a saucer shaped hole about two inches less deep than the height of the root ball, and about five times the diameter of the root ball. Add about three tablespoons of 0-45-0 to the bottom of the hole and work it into the soil. Set the plant firmly in the center of the saucer and backfill with the crumbled dirt that came out of the hole. Don't add other amendments such as sand, peat moss, or compost to the soil. Firm the soil around the plant, water well and mulch.

The eight cultivars that grow best for me at The Blessed Earth Farm, and in other gardens I've had in this area, are *Roseum Elegans*, which is true lavender; and *English Roseum*, which is a lighter lavender color, and a smaller plant at maturity with smaller trusses; *Nova Zembla* is the best red I've found for Spartanburg. *Anna Rose Whitney* is a deep pink, and *Cynthia* is a medium pink, both are so beautiful that it makes your heart leap just to look at them. *Ice Cube* and *Catawbanese Album* are the two best whites. *Lee's Dark Purple* is almost black, and it is great planted with the white *Catawbanese Album*. These two huge plants bloom at the same time, and the contrast of colors makes a fantastic show.

I don't eat sausage biscuits anymore. My doctor convinced me a few years ago that orange juice, cereal, and skim milk are better choices for an old guy; so, I don't go to Hardees anymore. But, it was there that Bob Edge and I started a friendship that continued in the garden. I might have added a bit of cholesterol to my veins with the sausage biscuits, but that's okay, because otherwise I would have never met Bob.

The rhododendrons are in bloom, and Bob will probably walk with me tomorrow as I walk my garden path down to see them, and he'll correct me if I say the wrong name for one of the cultivars. Bob, I can still use a few pointers: you'll always be the master.

Prelude to *Don't Forget to Wash Behind Your Ears*

The telephone may be one of the most intrusive inventions to ever to come along. Maybe one day someone may invent something more intrusive, but I can't imagine what it will be. We got our first telephone before we got our first indoor plumbing. We got the telephone in 1940 when I was eight years old. We got the indoor plumbing a month or two before I finished high school, just as I was turning eighteen years old.

When we got our first telephone I was still young enough to play outside with my buddies. I would be outside, in the hot of an Alabama summer afternoon, playing cowboys and Indians and all dirty and sweaty when the telephone would ring. After a couple of minutes momma would stick her head out the back door and holler at me, "Come in and get cleaned up, company is coming, and don't forget to wash behind your ears." The company would have come whether or not we had had a telephone for them to call and let us know they were coming. In those days drop in company was the rule rather than the exception, because not many people had telephones.

The difference was that they would have found me sweaty and dirty from playing cowboys and Indians with my friends, and I wouldn't have had to take a bath and stand inspection to be sure I had washed behind my ears before they arrived.

Many times as Miss Beth and I cleaned up the garden and ourselves when we knew people were coming I thought about these little incidents from my childhood and how much easier it was for me to clean up one little boy than it was for us to clean up two acres of ornamental gardens, and ourselves, for company. Sometimes we got in such a rush that I forgot to wash behind my ears. Sorry about that, Momma.

DON'T FORGET TO WASH BEHIND YOUR EARS
Written Summer 2000

Miss Beth and I like to have visitors come to The Blessed Earth Farm. We especially enjoy it when some organization sets up a little tour on Saturday or Sunday to bring a group to see us: the way the Spartanburg Men's Garden Club did last Sunday afternoon.

We work hard the few days before a tour comes, getting our gardens ready. We try to pull up, dig out, or prune away our mistakes before visitors show up. Leastwise if we know they're coming we do. Sometimes people show up unexpectedly and we enjoy them too, but they may have to look at the garden in its *work clothes*, instead of in its dressed up *Sunday-go-to-meetin' best suit*.

The couple of days before our guests arrive Miss Beth and I are busy mowing grass and bush hogging the parts of the pasture up around the house. We trim the woody ornamentals, dead head the annuals and herbaceous perennials, and pull the weeds out of the gardens.

If the season is dry we get the irrigation system in high gear, so when the guests arrive the garden is damp and the plants look like they've just experienced a refreshing summer rain. Miss Beth always has some homemade lemonade and iced tea, and some cookies and maybe some muffins, laid out on a fresh tablecloth on one of the shady decks, for a little cooling refreshment. Touring gardens is hot work and the cooling drinks disappear quickly. Unexpected visitors may have to make do with just iced tea.

In short we get rid of all the ugly we can, trash our mistakes, and put our best foot forward. I sometimes feel a little bit guilty about not letting guests see the garden in its overalls and brogans, but I guess it's okay everyone wants to put their best foot forward when company's coming.

Most of the time dressing up the garden is as simple as mowing, pulling weeds, dead heading and pruning to shape and tidy up plants, but sometimes it's as difficult as admitting you've had a failure, that you made a mistake, or that a part of the garden just let you down after all your hard work. It's always hard to make a major change in the garden—as it is in your life—but sometimes circumstances get out of control.

One of the hardest things for new gardeners to learn is that sometimes things simply go wrong in the garden. Plants, like people, can be mysterious in their growth and development. Some plants grow healthy and vigorous; then again the same kind of plant, same variety, planted a few feet away from the healthy plant, will mysteriously fail to develop the way nature and the gardener intended. When plants have been carefully planted and nurtured, there are usually two basic reasons why they don't develop as they should.

Reason number one is that the wrong plant was planted in the right place or that the right plant was planted in the wrong place. I love the big blue delphiniums that I see in pictures of British gardens and in the 'north of the Mason-

Dixon Line' garden catalogs. I've been trying to grow them for years, but our climate is all wrong for them and they just *ain't* going to thrive in South Carolina heat and humidity. There are some delphiniums that grow well here, but they don't make the dramatic show that the big blue ones do. And, I'm just stubborn enough to keep wasting my money and my time, trying to grow the big blue kind, so that people will think I'm as smart as my cousins in England, who grow such wonderful gardens. I could name a lot of plants that fall into the category of plants I love and try to grow, but fail. This comes under the heading of *knows better, but just ain't got enough sense to stop.*

Reason number two that a plant doesn't grow right is: *I just don't know.* Beware young gardeners of the "know it all" gardener who has an answer for all your questions. Run fast in the other direction. Sometimes in spite of all your knowledge, skills, and loving care, things go wrong in your garden—just as they do in your life. Sometimes you have to say the three hardest words in any language "I don't know".

I wish I could learn this lesson and quit beating myself over the head for those things that go wrong in my garden and in my life.

Sometimes when you've worked and planned and done your best and still a section of your garden doesn't turn out right you just have to dig it up throw it on the compost pile and start over again. It's painful, but it's part of gardening. It's the same way with the bad habits in your life. Sometimes you have to dig them out of your life and throw them on the compost pile. It's painful, but it's a part of life.

Prelude to *Me and Jess and the Geezer Brigade*

I wrote Me and Jess and the Geezer Brigade *sometime in 2002. Most of the things I tell about in the story happened in the mid 1990s. Jess was a young eighty-three or eight-four back then. Today he's a young ninety-one and still going strong. I wouldn't dare divulge his wife, Allene's, age, but I think I can safely say that she isn't far behind Jess and she keeps up just fine.*

Jess is adamant that his longevity and good health is due to eating a cup of blueberries on his cereal each morning. He and Allene grow the blueberries and freeze them so that Jess can have his magical fountain of youth formula each morning all year round. I wouldn't venture an opinion of whether the blueberries are the reason Jess is so active and healthy at ninety-one, but it's hard to argue with success.

Jess and Allene came to visit the other the other day. It's blueberry season so they brought Miss Beth and me a big sack of blueberries. I ate them on my cereal every morning as long as they lasted. Hey, is that a bit of youth I feel creeping into my body?

Other than family, the greatest blessings of my life are the many friends I've made.

ME AND JESS AND THE GEEZER BRIGADE

Written sometime in 2002

One of the first friends I made after moving to Spartanburg was Jess Taylor. A few years later Jess doubled my pleasure in our friendship by marrying Allene Wood.

Jess and I met through our mutual interest in gardening. When I moved to Spartanburg I was looking around for ways to make friends in a new town, and naturally I looked in the direction of gardening organizations, because that's where my interests were. I registered into the Master Gardener class that started a few weeks after I moved to town.

The first time I saw Jess Taylor was when he stepped to the front of the Master Gardener class to teach plant propagation. With his ruddy cheeks and twinkling blue eyes, Jess looked like a Hollywood director had cast him in the part of a movie gardener. He had the erect posture and athletic carriage of an outdoorsman, and his scuffed shoes and rough clothing attested that he was a *working* gardener. When Jess began to speak, he dissolved any doubt that might have lingered in anyone's mind that he was a Master Gardener. Jess knew how to propagate plants, and he knew how to teach other people to propagate plants.

It hadn't been long since I had quit the business of being a busy business executive, and I still had a bad case of type-A personality. That day in Master Gardener class, Jess got me excited about plant propagation, and when a type-A personality gets excited about a project there are no boundaries, the sky's the limit. In order to have plenty of room to practice my newly learned craft of propagating plants, I rushed out and bought a little farm, which I named The Blessed Earth Farm, and seven years later it became my home.

I could tell endless stories about the many days that Jess and I spent, with a band of other geezers, working with Harold Hatcher at Hatcher Gardens. Today it's known as Hatcher Gardens and Woodland Preserve, and they've got everything managed and organized, but in those days seven or eight old geezers, led by Harold Hatcher did most of the work on a catch as catch can basis.

I could tell you more stories about the days Jess and I climbed in my old Ford pickup and rode the back roads of the Upstate of South Carolina, and the Western North Carolina mountains, ostensibly on the business of finding plants or picking up supplies for Hatcher Gardens, but really just enjoying each other's company and telling the war stories of our lives, like old men are prone to do.

But those stories can wait for another day. This story is about Jess Taylor and Allene Wood, two people who met, fell in love, got married and built a beautiful home on Lake Saranac. They then surrounded the home with a beautiful garden, and they did all this at an age when most people are making plans to move into a retirement home.

After the house was finished, Jess and Allene began building the gardens. Most days they climbed in their pickup and scoured the mountains of Western North Carolina, looking for just the right stones to outline the paths and to build the walls. They bought a small concrete mixer and Jess mixed the mortar to lay the stones, and he and Allene placed them carefully, taking full advantage of the rugged rocks.

With the infrastructure in place, they began to plant the many woody ornamentals that Jess had propagated—blueberries, wygelia, hydrangea, azalea and many more varieties to line the paths that they had built. Then they added perennials for color.

The back garden that runs down to Lake Saranac is sunny and mostly lawn, and a few years ago, they started a rose garden there in the back garden. But, like most people who start rose gardens, Jess and Allene soon tired of the constant attention the roses demanded and began thinking about changing it to something different.

Allene had the idea to plant the rose garden in wildflowers that like sunny locations. So in late winter they went down to Tony Hollifield's Piedmont Farm and Garden Store and bought about $10.00 worth of wildflower seed, which they sowed in the fast-disappearing rose garden.

The seed germinated and this summer the area is a colorful delight of cosmos, California poppies, bachelor buttons and many other bright blooms, blowing in the gentle breezes off Lake Saranac.

I really miss the days working with the geezer brigade at Hatcher Gardens and I miss the long lazy days that Jess and I spent riding the country roads in the big blue pickup truck, embellishing our life's adventures ... but our lives have moved on. We both have lost wives and remarried since we first met and our wives have cleaned us up and changed our geezer ways.

I told Jess that we shouldn't have married women who are smarter than us.

Prelude to *The Bullfrog and Magical Gardens*

I've always liked "once upon a time stories," because as a child I knew they were make believe and that they could tell about magic kingdoms, and fire-breathing dragons, and all other sorts of magical things. When I got to be grown, I still loved them, but they no longer started with the words "once upon a time." They started with words like "It was a dark and stormy night", and the stories were called fiction, which also meant that they could still tell about all sorts of things that didn't usually happen in real life. Well, I guess they happened, but not in nearly as a dramatic a way as the fiction setting of the books. The beauty of a book is that one can entertain one's self for hours on end without anything but the book: no people and no equipment required and, if the book is good, then happiness and satisfaction are guaranteed.

As I got a bit older my favorite stories were history, biographies and autobiographies. I liked these books because they took me to the places where the great men and women of history had been. I could tread the floors of Mount Vernon with George Washington, and sit with Thomas Jefferson in the White House as he planned the Lewis and Clark expedition. I could put myself in the middle of all sorts of true, historical events and sit and walk by the sides of the giants of history ... and all I needed was a free library card.

As I became more discriminating in my reading, I learned that there was a lot of fact in the "once upon a time" stories and a lot of fiction in the best researched of the histories, biographies and autobiographies. But that's the way with most everything in life ... a bit of fact and a bit of fiction, and we have to learn to live with it.

I always had a desire to find a once upon a time story that was truth: all truth. I never found that story so I decided to write one of my own. The Bullfrog and the Magical Garden *is the one "once upon a time" story that is truth—well ... there could be a bit of poetic license.*

The Bullfrog and The Magical Garden
Written Summer 2003

Once upon a time there was a giant bullfrog that stood watch over a magical garden on the eastside of Spartanburg City. Although the bullfrog was nearly seven feet tall he was a good and kind frog, who welcomed all who came in peace to enjoy the mystical garden. All were welcome to the garden except for the few who were evil and came to harm the garden. The evil ones were exorcised from the frog's domain by one mighty blow of his huge hind leg.

Then one night many evil men came in force and overpowered the mighty frog and stole him from the garden. The frog was gone for many days and there was much sadness in the garden. The flowers hung their heads and cried, the sturdy woody ornamentals wept, and the beautiful fescue lawn turned brown, and lo the tears of the shrubs and flowers could not revive the lawn. But saddest one of all was the owner of the garden, Sandy Sanders, a man of jolly disposition. He continued to cultivate his garden, but his feet dragged as he moved back and forth through the magical garden and the smile was gone from his face. He was lacking some of his usually abundant enthusiasm. The garden was just not the same without his friend, the frog, whom he sorely missed.

Then one morning the frog was found. Sandy went immediately to claim his long lost friend. He returned the frog to the place of prominence at the front of the garden and anchored him in a ton of concrete so that evil men could never again steal the frog from his home, and he could remain guardian of the garden.

This fairytale is essentially true. I have taken a bit of poetic license, but not enough to change the essence of the story. Sandy Sanders has created a garden fairyland around his home. It's filled with beauty and whimsy. Walking Sandy's garden is an experience of subtle surprise and wonder.

There are no paths, as we usually think of paths in a garden. There are openings between the plants that wander hither and thither like a garden maze where the visitor can wander for hours and always find something new to delight the senses. Sandy is a plant collector. He likes to haunt the garden centers of North and South Carolina, always looking for a new plant or ornament for his garden. He peruses the catalogs of the garden world, and he researches the vast horticulture literature for new plants and cultivars that will grow in our area.

When Sandy discovers a woody ornamental or an herbaceous perennial and brings it home he delights in finding just the right place in the garden for it, which is becoming more and more difficult. A few years ago Sandy ran out of room and purchased an overgrown lot next door. He cleared it and began to plant and cultivate, but the luxury of space in his garden was short lived. Now, the new plot of land is filled with plants and ornaments.

There are too many plants in Sandy's magic garden to even to begin to tell you about. One standout is the peonies. Peonies aren't easy to grow in our area, but Sandy has a great collection, which is thriving. Sandy has a love for rhododendrons and azaleas, and never passes up an opportunity to get a new cultivar. Camellias abundantly adorn the garden in all their winter color and glory. Sandy was one of the first fans of Encore azaleas and has one of the best collections I have seen. Recently, during an addition to the house, one of Sandy's prize camellias was threatened and in spite of the heroic efforts Sandy put forth the old and beautiful camellia could not be saved. I helped Sandy shed a tear over its demise.

Sandy's wit and whimsy is demonstrated throughout the garden in ornaments hidden among the plants. It takes some careful looking not to miss them. I won't tell you all the secrets, you may want to visit the garden, but look carefully among the azaleas and you'll see an alligator that is snapping at the seat of a man's pants. Sandy says this illustrates his feelings of all the years he spent in the business world, thinking that he was up to his—uh, well—you know, in alligators.

The nose (this is not a typo it is nose not rose) garden is a surprise we'll hold in reserve, but the name ought to whet your appetite and no it doesn't have to do with fragrance. One of the most beautiful features of the garden is the half-ton fountain made of granite that Sandy has recently installed, and there's much, much more to see in Sandy's magic garden.

Sandy is also one of the most enthusiastic Master Gardeners to ever pick up a hoe. He kicks off most of the Master Gardener classes with his wit, a weekly tip on great plants and how to be a better gardener. Sandy, through his enthusiasm for the Master Gardener organization, is probably the main reason that the classes are always full and there is a waiting list for next year's class.

Except for a small area of lawn, the driveway, and the walk from the driveway to the house, Sandy's entire property is garden. And, when I visit I'm always careful turning into the driveway. I ... not unrealistically ... expect I might find that Sandy is beginning to turn the driveway into garden—nah, Anne, his wife, would never let him get away with that. Would she?

Prelude to *A Wedding at The Blessed Earth Farm*

I'm a bit sentimental about weddings, and weddings in a garden bring tears of sentimental joy to my eyes just thinking about them. When my elder daughter, Betsy, decided to marry Paul Smith, and wanted to hold the wedding in the gardens of The Blessed Earth Farm, Miss Beth and I were delighted. Miss Beth is pretty sentimental also, but, unlike me, she goes out of her way to hide the fact.

Betsy and Paul's wedding was a bit fancier than mine and Miss Beth's had been at the farm. By the time Betsy and Paul married we had enlarged the house. Part of the enlargement was building the big all glass garden room onto the house. We had also developed about two acres of ornamental gardens around the house and built the two big decks around the pecan trees out front, so we were able to have the reception at the farm also. We had plenty of space and plenty of shade.

Miss Beth and all the ladies set up the food for the reception in the garden room. It was perfect for the food, because it's all glass and looks out on the gardens, and all the sissies could stay inside in the air conditioning and still enjoy the feeling of being outside. I set up the bar in the kitchen and we had big tin tubs of ice, soda pop beer and wine strategically placed around the gardens since it was August and hot. We didn't want anyone to get too thirsty in the Carolina August heat. The preacher was a lady and I noticed that even she enjoyed a couple of glasses of white wine.

Dress was very informal: Betsy was beautiful and Paul was handsome, and the guests although many had never met before got on well. Buster, our dog, who is still with us, had taken up at the farm just a few weeks before the wedding and he walked up and stood by the preacher just as I walked Betsy across the big deck to the smaller deck where Paul, the preacher and the groomsman and bridesmaid stood waiting for her. As I gave Betsy's hand to Paul, Buster turned and walked away with me. Buster provided a little merriment and some competition to the bride, but Betsy was more than up to it.

The wedding was informal and a lot of fun. Many of the guests didn't leave until well into the night, as the Hawaiian lanterns began to flicker to show that they were about out of oil—and I think it would be fair to say that some of the people were about as lit as the lanterns. The lanterns were about empty of oil, the tubs were empty except for some water from the melted ice and the bar was getting real low as most of the guests headed back to civilization. It was an informal wedding and lots of fun: the perfect kind of wedding for the gardens of The Blessed Earth Farm.

A Wedding at The Blessed Earth Farm
Written Summer 2002

We had a wedding in the gardens at The Blessed Earth Farm last Friday evening. My daughter, Betsy, was married. It was a small affair of only about fifty to sixty people: just family and a few close friends of the bride and groom.

About two months ago, Betsy told Miss Beth and me that she was going to get married and would like have the ceremony and reception in the gardens at The Blessed Earth Farm. We were flattered that she wanted to get married here at the farm. I've always thought weddings in gardens were a special thing. Miss Beth and I were married here about four years ago, but there weren't any gardens here then, and the big decks out front hadn't yet been built, so we got married on the little deck out back under the shade of the big white oak trees with just the wind chimes for music.

It was late May when Betsy talked to us about her wedding plans. It sounded easy then—the gardens were fresh, there had been some late spring rains and the weather was nice and cool. I can't imagine any circumstances that would have caused us to say no to Betsy's having her wedding here, but had I known that we were facing two months of almost constant ninety degree-plus heat and practically no rain, I might have at least thought about saying no.

This has been one of the toughest summers for gardening that I remember and I remember a lot of summers and a lot of gardens. The stress on the plants has been horrible and Miss Beth and I have had to use every trick that we've learned in our many years of gardening and studying to keep the gardens looking good for the wedding. Miss Beth has been deadheading perennials, butterfly bushes and other woody ornamentals almost full time, and I've been pruning out dead branches and pouring water to the gardens at the rate of about three inches a week—and that's a lot of water over two acres of ornamental gardens.

Even with all the water and the care that we've given the garden, we've had to remove several dead plants. This has been a killing summer for plants that didn't have time to establish good root systems before the heat and dry came, and that are borderline to the South Carolina summer heat when it comes with a vengeance, the way it has this year, and decides to remain long after the welcome mat has been jerked out from under it.

The rule of thumb, which most gardeners in the Piedmont follow, is that a garden needs an inch of water each week during the growing season. It really takes at least two inches of water a week in the weather we've been having lately; but, if you want the garden to look good, it takes a bit more than two inches when the thermometer is threatening to blow out the top everyday and the rains refuse to come. Deadheading is important in any weather, but it is a must in the raging heat we've had this summer and it's even more effective if you do a bit of light pruning as you deadhead. The light pruning along with plenty of water gives a plant the opportunity to rejuvenate itself instead of leaving the old growth to turn brown as the blazing sun scorches it day after day. But a word of caution here—don't prune even lightly unless you're going to irrigate heavily.

Anyway, Miss Beth and I have persevered and the gardens looked pretty good for the big event. I don't know how many plants we have in the gardens and in pots at The Blessed Earth Farm, but the number must run into the thousands. I learned from Miss Beth and Betsy though that a wedding isn't a wedding without some potted ferns. We probably have a couple of hundred ferns, but they're all planted in the ground and we needed two big potted ferns to sit on plant stands that were placed on each side of the preacher's podium.

Our good friend Louise Neal came to the rescue and loaned us two of the prettiest ferns I ever laid my baby blues on. Louise and her husband Bill own Green Pond Nurseries a few miles up the way on Switzer Green Pond Road. It's the best place in the Upstate, in my opinion, to buy annual bedding plants. Louise is also expanding her selection of perennials each year and Green Pond Nurseries is fast becoming one of the premier perennial suppliers to gardeners in Spartanburg County.

The wedding went off just fine. The bride was beautiful, the groom was dashing and handsome, and may they live happily ever after. And, oh yes Louise I promise to get the ferns back to you sometime in the next couple of years they look real good out there on the deck under the big pecan tree.

Prelude to *Life's Way too Short to Hold Grudges*

There are many things in life that I don't understand, because they are beyond my intellectual capacity. I expect everyone falls into this category, at one time or another. There are also many things in life that I don't understand because they just seem foolish. I suspect that everyone falls into this category too. I expect the things in each category that people don't understand is different for each of us.

One of the things I have never understood is vandalism. I can understand robbery because those who commit robbery are taking something that they feel will benefit them. I don't condone it, but I can understand that at least the thief expects to benefit from the robbery. But I can't understand vandalism, the willful destruction of property which benefits no one. I have a couple of friends who are psychiatrists they've tried to explain to me the twisted minds of those people who commit acts of vandalism, but I simply can't understand that sort of mind. And, of course, there are much more serious crimes, such as the sexual abuse of children that seems to be so prevalent today that I can't even begin to get my mind around.

*Another act that I can't understand, because it seems so foolish is the act of holding a grudge. Holding a grudge hurts both of the parties involved. If someone or something causes you to want to hold a grudge it seems to **me** that you are only hurting yourself by doing so. The grudge just keeps eating away little pieces of you until you become a little less of a person than you would be otherwise. Or if you get into a serious grudge situation like the Hatfields and McCoys you can be instantly destroyed instead of wasting away a little piece at the time.*

When the grudge is with a person, you do all you can to resolve it, and if it can't be resolved then you put it aside and try to live with it. Grudges can be lived with and you can continue or discontinue the relationship. If the grudge is with an organization where you don't have a chance to resolve it then put it way back on the back burner and forget it. Don't let the grudge change your life.

The essay below is written about my relationship with my brother. We were so different and we disagreed on so many things that we could have held grudges against one another for our entire lives, but we didn't. It's also about how I could have held a grudge against the giant government department: the Social Security Department, but in doing so I wouldn't have hurt anyone but myself. The Social Security people wouldn't have noticed no matter how much I ranted and raved.

LIFE'S WAY TOO SHORT TO HOLD GRUDGES
Written Winter 2003

My only brother died a few weeks ago after a long illness. He fought the heart problems that had plagued him for twenty-five years with determination and courage. He was sixty-seven when he died. I'm three years older. I guess it's natural that I've been thinking a little more about mortality since his death.

I've always faced aging and mortality pragmatically. It's never bothered me when I turned another decade on the calendar. I remember forty years ago when my friends and I were turning 30. Most of them cringed at the idea, but I hardly noticed, and forty was a trauma for most of my friends, but that passing milestone didn't bother me either. Around the forty mark some of the guys started experimenting with hair growing chemicals and the gals used liberal amounts of hair coloring chemicals, but the fact that I was bald with little more than white fringe around the sides of my head, didn't bother me at all.

I tried to face aging by exercising regularly, by eating healthy foods and keeping my weight somewhat in line. I ignored the cosmetic approach to looking younger and just aged naturally; that fits the way I try to live: as simply and naturally as possible. My generation has now reached an age where all but the vainest have opted out of cosmetic fixes and fashionable clothes, and turned to the comfortable. There comes a time, if you live long enough, when old is going to get you anyway so you might as well relax, ignore the aches and pains and limitations, and enjoy it.

I noticed sixty-five because I finally got to start collecting all the hard earned dollars Social Security had deducted from my paycheck down through the years and invested in low-yield government bonds. I'm glad I don't hold grudges; this would have been a big one. I got to collect the maximum of about $1,050.00 a month from Social Security. I sat down at my desk one day right after I received my first Social Security check and did a bit of figuring. I compared the money I paid into Social Security with the return I made on my private investments. I figured that if I had been able to put the money I paid into social security into private investments and had realized 8% a year return on it the amount I would have had around $1,000,000 when I was 65. If I had then elected to invest it in government insured securities, ten year U.S. Treasury bonds or notes, I could have made a five percent return or about $50,000 a year ... considerably more than the $12,600 a year that Social Security is paying me, in fact about four times what Social Security is paying me. And the $1,000,000 would still be there for my children to inherit when I die.

As it is the money I paid into Social Security will be gone when I die. My good friends up in Washington spent it before they got it. So, I had a little resentment when I turned 65, but I got over it in a few days. I looked at the results of my private investments, which had averaged about ten percent over the years and was grateful that Social Security hadn't had all my money to manage. I had to look hard to find the silver lining, but I did. It's usually there if you get up and look for it instead to sitting down and feeling sorry for yourself.

The time just before bedtime, between 10:00 and 11:30, belongs to me. I love the music of the 1930s, 40s and 50s so I put on a set of headphones and sit outside or in the dimly lighted garden room, depending on the weather, and listen to the music I like so much, and I think. I usually have a little toddy or two to help my thinking along.

I've written a lot of essays during these sessions and the next morning I put them down on paper and polish them up. I don't discipline or limit my thinking during my thinking time. I let my mind find its own way along the paths of its complex structure, but it normally lights on one train of thought: one that usually surprises me. Then, it works on developing the thought into something that I can sometimes use.

Several times since my brother died, my mind has found its way down the path of our lives. We were as different as daylight and dark, so it would have been easy for us to blow up at one another and hold grudges. However, we were close as children and we remained close as adults. When we disagreed as children the result was usually a quarrel and sometimes a fistfight, but Momma was there to referee. When we disagreed as adults without Momma there to referee, we agreed to disagree and, we went on about our lives, without any significant disruption to our relationship as brothers. I'd hate to belong to a family that always agreed on things. I'd also dislike belonging to a family that held long-term grudges.

Life's pretty short and life at its longest is too short to hold grudges—even against Social Security—most especially at your brother.

Prelude to *I Was Finished With August on July 31ˢᵗᶜ*

From the time I quit the world of the busy business executive on December 31, 1988, until my cancer grounded me in November of 2007, I spent the majority of my time outside. It was probably the best time of my life. Not many people have the privilege of doing pretty much what they want to do for almost twenty years of their life. Even shortly facing a certain death, I still believe that I have been one of the most blessed men alive. In the twenty years since I left the business world, I've tried to live my life by the seasons and the calendar instead of by a watch and an appointment book. It wasn't always possible, but much of the time I succeeded.

I did some teaching and I served on several volunteer boards including the local Habitat for Humanity board, which is one of the most worthwhile organizations with which I have had the privilege to be associated. Most of my time, however, was spent outside in all kinds of weather. I loved to be outside on cold rainy days in December. I enjoyed the beautiful, delightful days of October when the sky was so blue I thought I could dive into it like a swimming pool, and the temperature was just right for doing those difficult physical jobs that, if started in the hot days of summer, sent you to sit in the shade of the big white oaks every thirty minutes or so.

I once wrote essays about each month of the year. I don't know why exactly now, but it seemed like a good idea at the time. I'm sure I have them filed away somewhere in my computer, but I haven't read them in years. I did dig out two for this book. One essay is about my least *favorite month of the year. The other is about October which ties with April as my favorite month of the year. I always like to get the bad behind me first so let's start with my least favorite month.*

I WAS FINISHED WITH AUGUST ON JULY 31ˢᵀ

Written August of 1997

August is the height of the dog days of summer as the Dog Star, Sirius, gets out of bed with the sun each morning. When I was a child, infections and digestive diseases ran rampant, especially in children who were too young to have built up resistance to these diseases.

When I was a boy, the old folks used to tell us that if you were cut or scratched or wounded in any way that broke the skin, during the dog days of summer the wound would not heal and it was likely to get infected—causing you to lose a finger or a limb or your life. And, they warned us to be careful of what we ate to be sure it was not "tainted" in anyway. They were right, of course, in that time before there were medicines to control infections, and before refrigeration was common, the sultry time of the summer—known as dog days—was the peak danger time for food poisoning and for infection.

Many children died in their second summer; these *knee* babies had not yet developed immune systems to handle food that was even just a little tainted; even the most vigilant mother could not always know if the food she was giving her baby was slightly spoiled. And the smallest scratch could become infected, and without the antibiotics we have today, a scratch could become quite serious before anyone recognized that it was a problem.

The old folks' warnings against animal bites and scratches during these hot July and August days were dire indeed. It was a time when mad dogs roamed our world. Maybe they didn't say exactly that, but it's what my eight year old ears heard. Anyway, what they said and the way they said it got my attention. I would look four times behind every bush as I moved about the land, especially if I had to be out after dark for any reason. I expected that behind each tree or shrub, I might encounter a big ugly dog with fierce red eyes, long sharp fangs glistening in the moonlight, and slobbering white froth at the mouth—ready to leap for my throat. I would wonder, in my eight year old imagination, if I could grab him around the neck as he leaped for my throat, and choke him to death with my bare hands before he could bite me. I think I saw too many Tarzan movies with Tarzan choking lions to death with his bare hands. I wondered if the bubbling froth would infect me with his madness, even if I succeeded in killing him before he bit me. These are the things of a boy's nightmares.

August is my least favorite month. There's not much going on in the garden. The summer vegetables are done except for some stray butterbeans and peppers here and there along the rows, and maybe a tomato once in a while from a vine that the early blight passed up in its rampage through the crop. The perennials, even the dauntless roses, are faded and drooping in the hot sultry sun. The brave annuals are losing their luster, but they will all perk up and regain their beauty when the cool nights of September have chased the parched world of August away.

The spent vegetable plants have to be removed from the garden, or turned under with the plow to add compost to the soil. The garden needs to be prepared to receive the seeds and sets of the fall vegetables, which should be planted before the end of the month. Following the tiller all day, getting this job done, with the searing white August sun beating down mercilessly out of the hot blue sky, is not one of my favorite jobs. Course, it adds a bit of fun when you can stop working for a while and cut a sweet ripe watermelon to slake your thirst, but then August will be about the end of watermelon and cantaloupe for another year.

The cows move listlessly over the pasture, seeking enough nourishment in their parched world to survive. Nothing much moves in the heat of the day except a few butterflies, a hummingbird here and there, and a carpenter bee comes by now and again—his short, stubby wings buzzing desperately to keep his big barrel body airborne. If you want to get some activity going, about the only sure fire way I know of is to set out a picnic lunch in the shade of a big tree and in August the yellow jackets will come by the millions.

All in all, it pushes me to find anything much to recommend August.

Prelude to *I'm Not Finished with October—Just Yet*

Many people who have read most of my work tell me that I'm not Finished with October—Just Yet, *is their favorite of all my works. I like it, but in a lot of ways it falls short of being my favorite. I think the thing that attracts most people, including me, to the little essay is the nostalgia it conveys of the gentle days of autumn ... the bridge between the hot days of summer and the approaching harsh winter days.*

The autumn of the year is naturally a time of nostalgia. It is a transition period when the warm summer is changing to dark and dreary winter. It seems that I can leave the windows open and go to bed on October 31st with the sky full of stars and brisk temperatures and be waken by rain beating on the tin roof in the early morning hours of November 1st, causing me to jump out of the bed and start closing windows, slamming them in a frantic hurry before I wind up having to do a lot of mopping.

After dressing and taking care of the early morning chores, I sit by the fire gazing out the window with a steaming cup of black coffee, watching the pouring rain and wondering what happened to the gentle October that was here when I went to bed last night.

I guess I was especially moved by the nostalgia of the autumn of 1997. My wife of forty six years had died of cancer on my birthday April 4th in the springtime of 1997. Not only was this October the transition period of the year, but it was a major transition period of my life.

I'M NOT FINISHED WITH OCTOBER—JUST YET

Written October 1997

October is my favorite month, except maybe for April. I've never been able to decide whether I like April or October better. What I'd really like is a year made up of six months of April and six months of October. But I guess then I'd miss the cold of winter and the hot of summer.

I do know that in another sixteen days October will end and we'll be rushing toward winter. And in winter, as I sit by the fire warming my hands after a few cold hours in the garden, I'll long for the lazy, languorous, golden days of October. I'm not ready to leave those golden days behind. Not just yet.

I want the color of October to last just a little longer. I've not had enough of the electric blue of the October sky. I want more of the glory colors of the sweet gum, and the deep, dark, burgundy of the black gum trees. I'm not ready for the brilliant yellow leaves of the hickory to go sailing off on the winds of November. I'm not ready for Jack Frost to turn the brilliant orange and yellow and purple blooms of my chrysanthemums to dirty brown. I'm not finished with the colors of October. Not just yet.

I don't want the sounds of October to fade. October is the final month until March that I will hear the indolent, slothful humming of the bumblebee as it searches for those last blossoms—blossoms which are now so sparse as to make its work tedious. In October the lawn mower's angry buzzing elopes with the last of the summer grasses; the mower's dying gasp is a loud clanking noise, like a knight in rusted armor as I push it into the barn for the last time of the season. I won't hear the steady, powerful pulling sound of the rotor-tiller's motor, or the high stringent sound of the string trimmer, until winter has passed and spring has come again. And when October is passed, the birds will spend their days in the brush, which shelters them from winter's wind and snow, and their sweet singing will no longer be heard upon the land.

I'm not finished with the sounds of October. Not just yet.

Nor do I want the tastes of October to vanish. Yesterday I walked to the arbor and picked the last of the muscadines. The taste was bitter sweet with the poignancy of being the last until next September. On the way back to the house, I picked up the first of this year's pecans and experienced the mellow flavor of the fleshy meat as I ate the tender new nut. October brings so many tastes; the sugary taste of the first sweet potato pie; the hauntingly, nutty flavor of turnip and collar greens now seasoned by the first frost; the clean taste of fresh cut broccoli, cabbage, and cauliflower; and the first pumpkin pie—mushy, syrupy, and spicy beyond belief. I'm not finished with the tastes of October. Not just yet.

And I'm not ready for the smells of October to be wafted away upon the winds of winter. I'm not done with the nostalgic feelings that explode in my brain when the first smell of hardwood burning in the fireplace reaches my nostrils. I'm not ready to release, for another year, the rich, earthy odor of soil as the summer crops are turned under. I don't want to give up for another year the smell of ripe red apples being crushed to make apple butter, apple sauce and apple cider. I'm not finished with the smells of October. Not just yet.

And finally, I'm not ready for the feels of October to flee into the quaking desolation of the dark winter. Just last week I felt the first cool breeze against my cheek, the breeze that told me that October would not be with me much longer. I'm not ready to release the comforting feeling of the warm October sun as I find a place against the south wall of the barn, where the wind can't reach me, while I shell and eat those first pecans, which along with the last of the scuppernongs, a tender new turnip and a slice of new cabbage are my lunch for this October day. I'm not ready yet to swap the sensation of crisp, cool, clear morning air, as I step out the door at daylight, for the cutting, cruel winds of November. And, please don't make me give up the spring in my step as I feel the bracing crispness of October, for the leaden lag in my step as I reluctantly push myself away from the warmth of the fire to do those outside chores in the garden and around the farm that must be done most days, no matter the weather. I'm not finished with the feels of October. Not just yet.

Oh Lord, if you could just let October last a little longer, I'd be grateful, but You've got the universe to run, which is a big job even for You, I expect. So just forget I asked and I'll be thinking of some of the good things that happen in winter and before I know it spring will be here and then summer and then another October, for I guess I'm just about finished with this one.

Prelude to *Remembering Autumns Past*

Remembering Autumns Past *doesn't need much explanation. It's pretty straight forward. The essay tells the memories of a boy who is now an almost old man: older than the old man in the story. I'm writing this in the autumn of 2007, ten years after I wrote* Remembering Autumns Past.

I expect I woke up one cool morning in September when we had opened up the house the day before, and I had to go looking for some warmer clothing—instead of doing the unspeakable of closing the windows and turning the thermostat to heat.

I most likely made a cup of coffee and sat down at the computer just to see what would happen, and Remembering Autumns Past *was the result. Anyway I'm glad to have those memories and I hope you enjoy remembering them with me.*

REMEMBERING AUTUMNS PAST

Written Autumn 1997

I like the change in seasons. It seems to me that it's like stepping into a new world each time we go from summer to autumn to winter and then to spring. No matter how boring our lives, the change from one season to another seems to put an extra zing into our steps. I like it when the seasons change suddenly: none of this gradual stuff for me. After a series of hot days that have lasted all summer I like to wake up one morning when the over night temperatures have dropped enough that I have to go to my extra clothes closet looking for an old sweater or sweatshirt. After daylight when the sun begins to warm mother earth this garment can be cast aside, and that night a quilt will feel good on the bed.

Good snuggling weather.

I think the change from summer to autumn is my favorite change of seasons, although the change from winter to spring runs nose-to-nose with it at the finish line. When I was a youngster the change from summer to fall was a time of preparation for the coming winter and a time for the celebration of harvesting the crops. It was a busy season. All the seasons were busy, but autumn was perhaps the busiest of all.

Today we have little need to prepare for winter. We set the thermostats in our homes from cool to heat, retrieve our winter clothes from storage, and do a few more simple tasks. We no longer need to store up food and fuel for the long winter months, and we no longer have a reason to celebrate the harvesting of the crops. We miss the fun of going to the woods behind a team of big red mules—frost covering the ground like snow—to cut wood for the winter's fuel.

When I was a boy, about this time of year, my grandpa, Mr. Willie Tankersley, would hitch the two big red mules, Dan and Red, to the wagon. We would load a couple of axes, a cross-cut saw, and a go devil in the wagon and head off across the fields to the woods on the far side of his little farm. We spent the day cutting down trees with axes. We cut oak and hickory for burning in the fire places and pine to use in the cook stove. After cutting the trees down with axes we then cut them into the right lengths for their ultimate use with the cross-cut saw.

We used a two man cross-cut saw with a handle at each end. I took one end and the old man, Paw Paw, took the other end. There was a lot of good natured yelling back and forth like, "Quit riding the saw and pull." "If you don't stop riding that saw I'm going to eat your dinner." Good natured yelling of this sort helped the job go faster, especially in the later morning when the frost had melted and jackets had given way to undershirts. Work time was the only time I was allowed to be the old man's quasi-equal and kid back and forth with him. All other times he was the man in charge and I was the boy he was in charge of.

After the logs had been cut to the right length the go devil was used to split them into the right size for burning. Several were always preserved whole to use as back logs. We then loaded the wood into the wagon and Dan and Red hauled the heavy loads to the house. Dan and Red had been staked out grazing in between hauling loads, but they earned their keep. The loads of green wood, especially the oak and hickory, made the old wagon creak under their weight. It took several days and lots of loads of wood during the fall to cut and haul enough wood for the winter. Once the wood was brought to the wood pile at the house, there was more work to be done. It had to be stacked so that it could cure without getting too wet if we had heavy fall rains. It was hard work, but the light hearted good natured competition and a little good natured fussing and cussing back and forth made the days slide by like eating boiled okra. I had to be careful about my cussing, but the old man could say about anything he wanted to as long as there were no women folk around.

During the summer we had picked, canned, and dried vegetables. In the fall in addition to cutting, hauling, and stacking wood we had to dig and mound sweet potatoes so that they would last through the winter—and hopefully through the next summer into August when the next crop would come in.

In early September we put in the collards and cabbage. These would often last through the winter unless we had a particularly hard winter. When the first hard freeze came it was time to kill hogs and preserve the meat. All the things we did in the fall time of the year in order to eat and stay warm in the winter, were grueling work, but as we worked, we dreamed of a kitchen warmed by the wood stove and fresh pork loin chops with baked sweet potatoes, greens, and corn bread; and of the wind whistling around the house as we ate in the warm kitchen.

The days passed quickly from fall to winter. There were also winter chores, but we had a lot of time to sit around the fire, eat parched peanuts and tell stories. Some of the real master story tellers of the south have never written a story, and have never in their wildest dreams thought about publishing one. The world has lost a lot by these stories not being recorded.

By the days after Thanksgiving most of the work was done and since we didn't start preparing for Christmas until a few days before the big day there was usually time for a square dance. The neighbors were invited and Mr. Willie tuned up his fiddle; his daughter, Reba and his brother, Charlie, picked up their guitars; and Mr. Willie's son, Quinn, grabbed his mandolin. A few jugs were placed at strategic places around the house and barn where the women folks couldn't see them—oh they knew the jugs were there alright—it was okay as long as they couldn't see them. Along about dark, as the lamps and lanterns were lit, Mr. Willie would strike the bow to the fiddle and the music and dancing would start. If the jugs lasted until daylight the music and the dancing did too. It was a bunch of bleary eyed men and tired women who dragged home to do the morning chores of feeding the stock and milking the cattle, but it was a happy bunch of men and women.

Miss Beth and I live on a farm a little smaller that Mr. Willie's farm, and we live close to nature, but I'm grateful we don't have to do the hard work to prepare for winter that we did in those long ago days when I was a boy.

Still Miss Beth and I have spent a lot of time outdoors walking and gardening, so we notice the subtle change as the seasons move from one to the next. We've noticed already, even though fall has just begun, that the leaves of the big sycamores are brown and the tulip trees are showing a lot of yellow. As Miss Beth and I walked Otis and Spanky, our dogs, down through the woods along the creek this morning, I noticed that the sweet gum trees are beginning to show color. The sweet gum is the southern answer to the northern sugar maple. It's one of our prettiest trees in the fall with its myriad colored leaves. It would be nice if we could figure out a way to do away with the porcupine *eggs* it drops though. I have read that someone has done this, but I haven't been able to find this variety.

The limbs of the persimmon trees are hanging heavy with almost ripe persimmons and the leaves are a bright copper color. If I still hunted 'possum, a couple of weeks from now I'd be visiting the persimmon trees late in the night expecting to find a big, old, silver back possum up there enjoying his favorite food.

The herbaceous perennials—except for those such as the mums and asters and golden rod—that come into their own as fall deepens, are beginning to die back. And the deciduous shrubs—wygelia, forsythia and such—are beginning to drop their leaves. The tall needle evergreens—Leyland cypress and Carolina sapphire; and the broadleaf evergreens—Emily Bruner holly, the Savannah hollies, the fragrant ozmanthus, and the sasanqua and japonica camellias—are standing tall out front by the road. They'll give The Blessed Earth Farm a nice screen from passing eyes and northern winds all winter.

It won't be long until we'll feel the crunch of frost and frozen grass beneath our boots as we start our early morning walks with our dogs on the land that is The Blessed Earth Farm. We'll welcome that second cup of steaming coffee when we get back to the old farm house, as I sit thinking back to those years that used to be, when Mr. Willie and I harnessed Dan and Red to the double tree wagon and went to cut wood. I'll also be dreaming about those fresh pork chops and newly-dug, baked sweet potatoes my grandma fed us after a hard day's work of butchering hogs.

And I'll think about this special, sweet dying time of the year that we call autumn.

Mr. Willie and Miss Emily Tankersley

Mr. Willie and Miss Emily Tankersley

Miss Emily in the kitchen

Mary Alice, Archie, Dwayne and Winston Hardegree

David Archibald Hardegree

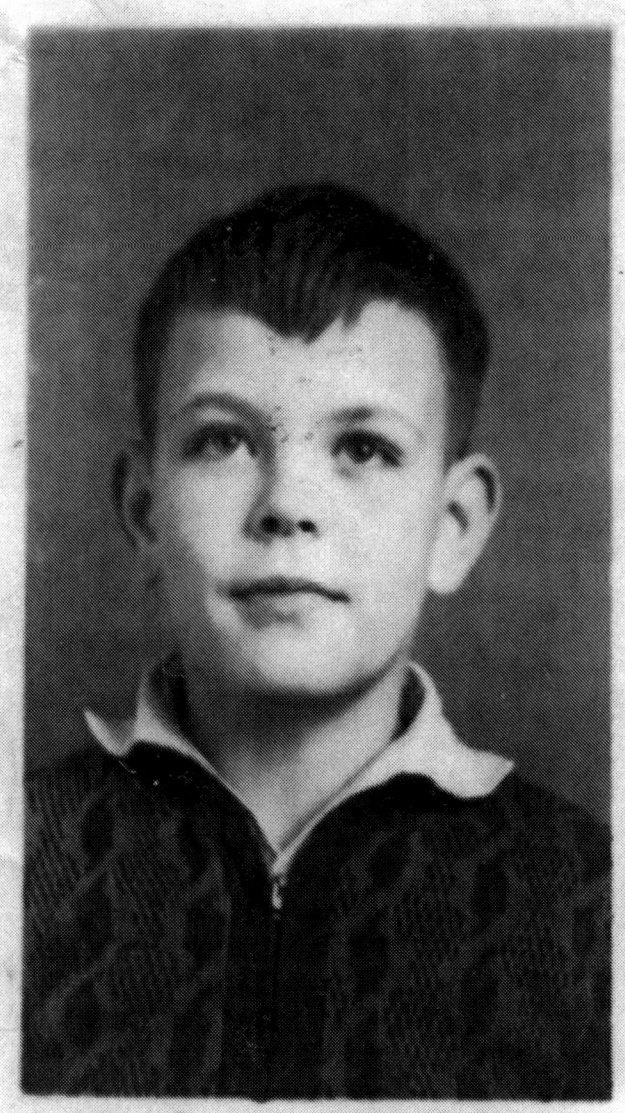

School Days
1941-42

Winston, the boy

Winston, the young "busy business executive"

The Blessed Earth Farm, early days

Elizabeth Sabin Hardegree
Miss Beth on her wedding day, September 1998

Winston walking the pasture with his son and several of his grandchildren

Winston and Miss Beth

Otis and Spanky

Queen Maggie

Winston with Spanky and Otis

The Blessed Earth Farm barn and gate to the pasture

Winston and Miss Beth

Miss Beth in the shade garden

Winston and Miss Beth

Winston in the garden

Prelude to *Beauty and Destruction: Joy and Despair*

Many people in the Upstate of South Carolina and Western North Carolina will long remember the ice storm of early December 2003. Most folks were without power for from two to seven days. A few very lucky people escaped losing power. The Blessed Earth Farm is in one of the most remote parts of Spartanburg County, we're at the end of the power lines and we usually suffer through these outages longer than most of the residents of the County. We were without power for a full week.

We had another ice storm in December of 2005, almost exactly two years after the one of 2003. The second storm didn't do as much damage as the first storm and we lost power for only five days. This is another of the inconveniences of living in the country. But, when Miss Beth and I relive the experiences of Little Miracles Happen Everyday, I'm not Finished with October, Red-Tailed Hawks and Baby Chicks, A Morning to Live For, *and several of the other stories in this book, we agree that we could never live anywhere else.*

Beauty and Destruction: Joy and Despair *tells of the beauty and joy that can be found even in destruction and despair. During the second ice storm my attitude was more like Spanky, Otis, and Buster's which was "come on let's play with the pretty ice and forget the destruction." I believe that if we have another bad one this would be my attitude again.*

BEAUTY AND DESTRUCTION: JOY AND DESPAIR

Written Winter 2003

I don't remember ever experiencing such opposing emotions at the same time as I did Thursday morning December 5, 2003, as daylight slowly exposed the world around The Blessed Earth Farm. Miss Beth and I woke, as is our custom, before daybreak, but this morning there was no comforting mug of steaming black coffee or nice warm air coming in through the furnace vents. We had lost our power the night before as the fury of the worst ice storm in my memory took our world in its icy grip, and I was too preoccupied with what sights the daylight would bring to fire up the camp stove we use in emergencies. I did take time to get our auxiliary butane heating system going, and Miss Beth got out the flashlights, lanterns and candles. She also got the reserve water we keep in bottles. Living out in the country we get our water from a well, and when the power goes off the electric pump quits working, and we are without water. We also keep a reserve of water in tubs for flushing toilets. When we have an outage of this caliber the power may be off for four to five days. This time, the damage was so wide spread it took seven days for the power to come back on.

We knew there was a lot of damage. I have impaired hearing and when I take my hearing aids out at night I don't think a firecracker exploding next to my ear would wake me. But, Miss Beth had heard the creaking, cracking, breaking and falling of limbs all during the night, while I slept soundly. In spite of that we weren't prepared for the war zone that daylight revealed. We stood in the glass garden room watching as a world of beauty and devastation slowly emerged from the long dark night. My emotions were all mixed up. My heart leapt with joy at the beauty of the ice sparkling like diamonds as far as our eyes could see. My stomach ached with despair as I witnessed the destruction of much of the beauty of the gardens of The Blessed Earth Farm which first I, and then after our marriage, Miss Beth and I together, had worked to create in the last eight years.

The twenty-five foot Leyland cypresses out front lay on the ground wounded and broken. The Carolina Sapphires were bent double, their tall pointed tops almost touching the ground. Emily Brunner and Savannah hollies, heavenly bamboo, and kiss me at the gate were splayed across the earth like kids making snow angels. The two decks out front that are built around the two big pecan trees were covered with the ice laden broken branches of the trees. One limb was sticking through the cover of the spa. Some of the limbs were a foot thick and twelve feet long.

As light brightened the day our spirits sank further into darkness as we walked around back and saw that one of the one-hundred year old white oak trees had split. One part of the four-foot diameter tree had fallen and crushed the front part of one of our two-story barns—the other half was leaning precariously over the new glass addition to the old farmhouse. We anxiously rushed around back where Otis and Spanky, our dogs, sleep in stables, snug in beds of fragrant cedar shavings. Buster, our other dog who lives in the house with us, ran happily alongside us licking the icicles and jumping the hurdles of debris that littered the driveway and paths. Otis and Spanky had escaped any injury and greeted us with joy, as they always do. They were ready for their breakfast and their romp through the pasture. Breakfast coming right up, but there would be no romp this morning. The dogs would have done fine with their four wheel drives, but our two wheel drives couldn't handle the slippery conditions.

My thought, as I saw the exhilaration of the dogs was that I had to get rid of my gut-wrenching despair and look at this beautiful morning of devastation through the happy eyes of the animals. But then they didn't have to worry about getting half of the huge white oak, hanging by its imagination over the house down, before it fell and crushed the house. I shouldn't have either.

Ricky Ellason, of Ellason Tree Service in Simpsonville, and his crew carefully worked the big tree down piece by piece. In the end there was no real reason for my anxiety; I could have been happy like Otis and Spanky and Buster and enjoyed the beauty of the winter wonderland.

The shade gardens, beneath the grove of huge white oak, tulip poplar, and hickory trees were so littered with the fallen limbs of the hundred year old trees—some of the limbs as large as an ordinary shade tree—that it was impossible to walk the paths to determine the damage to the woody ornamentals beneath them: plants that Miss Beth and I had collected and lovingly planted and tended.

The herbaceous perennials, ferns, hostas, toad lilies, bleeding hearts, blood root, woodland phlox and many others, are sleeping safely under the protection of the earth and the fallen leaves from the big trees. They should awaken next spring to bring beauty, but the broken woody ornamentals will take several years to regain their size and beauty.

Many visitors to The Blessed Earth Farm have admired the specimen winter honeysuckle, kiss me at the gate, (there's an essay about this beautiful shrub a little later in the book) that grew as big as a small bus at the corner of the tool house, and spread the fragrance of its light yellow blooms all over the area in February and March. The blooms and fragrance will not come this year. The big plant has more than fifty trunks growing from its roots, but all are broken back to the ground by a large limb that fell on it. It will grow once again and reach its previous glory, but not for a few years.

Miss Beth, the dogs and I are healthy, happy and digging out. We'll be awhile and we'll have to cancel the tours we have scheduled for The Blessed Earth Farm gardens this spring and summer. But, after seven days, the power is back on, life is returning to normal, and the gardens will bloom once again this spring although they will be blooming alongside a lot of destruction. And, I promise to be more like Spanky, Otis and Buster if this ever happens again. I can't leap debris anymore, but I can still lick icicles.

Prelude to *The Ludwicks: Super Volunteers*

Once in a while you meet people that you want to keep in your lives forever. You never know when and where this will happen.

Some of the new friends I made after moving to Spartanburg that you'll read about in this book were met in unexpected places. I met Bob Edge in a Hardees restaurant. There's a chapter on him in here. I met Sandy Sanders in the Master Gardeners class, but we spent time outside of class and became fast friends. There's a chapter on him in the book. The biggest surprise of all, however, is that I met my future wife, Miss Beth, whose story runs all through the book, in a Master Gardener class. She was the student; I was the teacher. Now our roles are reversed.

In the following chapter I tell about Bob, Jan and Kelly Ludwick. We had stand out volunteers in each Master Gardener class, but I think the Ludwicks, all three of them, are the most outstanding of the outstanding.

THE LUDWICKS: SUPER VOLUNTEERS

Written Autumn 2002

Master Gardener is indeed a respected title, but when I think about the contributions that the Ludwicks have made to the Master Gardener program and to Spartanburg County, I'd like to come up with a title that is even more respected to bestow upon them. I'd like to think of something really special, but the best I've been able to do is to give them the title of Super Volunteers. The Master Gardener program's slogan is "volunteers making the difference." The Ludwicks are super volunteers who make a huge difference.

The Ludwick family numbers three. Bob, the father, is the quiet one—he's a retired mechanical engineer. Jan, the mother, is the loquacious one—she's a retired registered nurse. Kelly, their adult daughter, is the one who steals my heart.

I first met the Ludwicks four years ago. It was about this time of year. Master Gardener classes were starting and, as monitor for the afternoon class, I received an unusual request. We have ten tables in the classroom and seat three people at each table on a first-come, first-served basis and then ask that people keep those seats for the seventeen weeks of the class. The unusual request I received was to reserve the back table by the door and that there would only need to be two chairs placed at that table.

Just before the first class started that fall afternoon Bob and Jan rolled Kelly's wheel chair to the reserved table in the back of the room by the door, and took the two chairs we had placed at the table for themselves. The room has two doors so Kelly could sit there in her wheel chair and not interfere with the ingress and egress of other class members. It didn't take long to know that the Ludwicks are people who show this kind consideration in all that they do.

Kelly has a B.A. in English and has done some editing for me on things I write, and she does a terrific job. Kelly was born with cerebral palsy, but she concedes nothing to her condition or to her wheelchair. She has stolen my heart with her outgoing, loving, and optimistic attitude toward life. Kelly participates fully in life, and in all the MG activities. A hug from her, always freely given, is enough to make me feel good for days, and I can sit and bask in the sunshine she radiates for hours.

The three Ludwicks studied hard and finished near the top of that year's class of sixty Master Gardener candidates. That, however, wasn't the end of the story, but the beginning. Each Master Gardener candidate, in addition to completing the classroom work and passing a three-hour final exam, is required to complete forty hours of volunteer time in one or more horticulture projects that benefit the community.

A couple of years before the Ludwicks enrolled in the Master Gardener class, the Garden Writer's of America had started a program called Plant-A-Row for the Hungry. This is a national program that encourages all vegetable gardeners to plant one extra row in their garden and to donate the vegetables grown on that row to feed the hungry and homeless in their communities. The Spartanburg Master Gardeners decided to go The Garden Writers one better and, in conjunction with Spartanburg Technical College, started a whole garden of rows for the hungry on Spartanburg Tech property. We named it the *Plant-A-Row for the Hungry Garden.*

The late Harry Miller, a Spartanburg Master Gardener, was the first manager of this project and he got it up-and-going. But, about the time the Ludwicks were finishing their Master Gardener class work, Harry's health had deteriorated to the point he had to give up the *Plant-A-Row for the Hungry Garden*, so Bob, Jan and Kelly volunteered to ramrod this project. The Ludwicks started managing the project in 2000, and that year the garden produced 14,792 pounds of fresh vegetables, all of which were donated to various "soup kitchens" to feed the hungry and homeless of Spartanburg County. In 2001 the production of the garden was 31,054 pounds.

The final figure for 2002 is not in yet, but Saturday before last, Bob, Jan and Kelly, along with their jolly band of volunteers, harvested one ton (that's 2000 pounds) of sweet potatoes bringing the total for 2002 to 30,005 pounds. When the Saturday harvest was done the total was nineteen pounds short of the ton of sweet potatoes. Jan wanted so much to reach the 2,000 pounds that she asked Ziggy Krawiec, one of the loyal volunteers in the Plant-A-Row project, to go back to the garden and find another nineteen pounds. (I know Ziggy was tired after digging potatoes all day so I'd like to check the supermarket sales for that Saturday to see if just maybe one of them might have made a single sale for nineteen pounds of sweet potatoes.) There are still turnips, collards, broccoli and cabbage to harvest this year so the final poundage will probably exceed last year's harvest.

Jan keeps an exacting journal of what's planted and when it's planted, and oversees and records the weighing of each pound harvested. She's as meticulous in keeping her journal as I imagine she must have been in keeping patient's charts when she was a nurse on active duty; so the Master Gardeners have an exacting record of the production of the *Plant-A-Row for the Hungry Gardens*.

Under the Ludwicks management the Plant-A-Row project has been expanded to three gardens. Any vegetable gardener knows that raising and harvesting vegetables is a labor-intensive endeavor. Raising and harvesting more than fifteen tons of vegetables to feed the hungry of Spartanburg County is a labor of love for the Ludwicks and the many Master Gardener volunteers who labor along with them under the hot South Carolina summer sun.

Both Bob and Jan were born and raised in Western Pennsylvania, and relocated to Spartanburg County about 28 years ago. Western Pennsylvania was the loser. Spartanburg County was the big winner. If Western Pennsylvania has anymore like the Ludwicks, just send them on down to South Carolina. We'll be happy to get them.

Prelude to *Our Beautiful Red Clay*

I have lots of fun talking with folks who move to Spartanburg County from other parts of the country, such as the Midwest, about our red clay soil. My advantage is that I have lived and gardened in the Midwest where almost anytime of the year, except deep winter, you can go out and dig a nice hole in which to plant a tree in about ten minutes. You can do that here also, but you have to do it in the wintertime unless you are working in an area that has been mulched for years, either by nature or by a savvy gardener.

Our soil is about as rich as you'll find anywhere in the world. The only fertilizer we use at The Blessed Earth Farm is the mulch that I describe in the essay below. Almost anywhere you decide to take a soil sample, unless the ground has been contaminated by oil or chemicals or some such villain, will come back with the printout that the soil needs very little if any amendments.

Of course, if you come from Minnesota you aren't accustomed to gardening in the winter. The climate just won't allow it, and besides you're too busy shoveling snow. But in the south, late autumn, all winter and early spring is the time to garden—except for vegetables. Remember, plant in the late fall and all winter and mulch in late winter and early spring, and if mulch becomes available during the summer spread it on the garden then also. In a few years you'll have a garden in which you can work year-round if you wish, but I'll bet that you'll still do your gardening in the winter time and sit under the big white oak trees and sip iced tea with your friends in the summer. You'll feel sorry for the poor old fellow out there trying to dig a hole and plant a woody ornamental in the summer. You might even have a bit of a laugh at his expense.

Our Beautiful Red Clay

Written Winter 1999

A lot of new people move to Spartanburg County each year, and many of them come from parts of the country that have very different soils and very different climates than we have here. I'm lucky to get to know many of the people who move to Spartanburg from all over this great country of ours, because of our mutual interest in gardening.

One of the subjects I teach in Master Gardener classes is *Soil Science and Plant Nutrition*. There are two questions most frequently asked by my new friends from other parts of the country, and even by some of my friends who have lived and gardened in Spartanburg for many years.

The first question is, "What do I do with this hard red concrete that you call soil?"

The next question is, "How do you manage to sit in the shade of those big white oak trees at The Blessed Earth Farm on these hot summer days, sipping iced tea and cogitating about life, and have the time to read all those books, and still have one of the prettiest gardens in the county, while I'm out here in the hot summer sun working my duff off trying to make a garden?"

The answer to these two questions is that in the Upstate of South Carolina you make your gardens in the late fall, winter and early spring, and, except for a little tidying up and irrigation as needed, you sit in the shade and read books and sip ice tea and visit with your friends in the summer.

Let's address the concrete red clay soil question first. You work concrete when it's soft instead of after it sets up, and you work our beautiful red clay while it's soft, which is in late fall, winter and early spring, not in the summer after it has set up. And, if you do your work right in the fall, winter and spring, you'll soon have soil that is soft and friable all year round.

Never try to start new gardens in the late spring, summer and early fall in Spartanburg County. It is next to impossible to dig a new garden during these times in our clay soil, unless you want to use blasting powder, In late fall, winter, and early spring, when the soil has been softened by rain and an occasional snow, digging a new garden is a task a child can accomplish. Late fall and early spring is also the time to plant perennials, and winter is the time to plant shrubs and trees in our area.

Before and after digging a new garden, and before and after planting a new garden, the garden should be mulched with organic matter such as leaves, pine straw, and grass clippings and this mulching should continue through the summer and after the garden is established.

Linda Cobb, in her recently published book, "My Gardener's Guide", writes about a visit that Michael Marriott, technical director for *David Austin Roses* in England made to her garden. Linda writes that Marriott made the statement that we Americans have much better soil than English gardeners. She then writes that, until he explained this statement, she had trouble believing it. I had a lot of trouble believing it, but Marriott's explanation makes a lot of sense.

He explained that our soil is better, because American gardeners mulch liberally, a practice that, according to Marriott, English gardeners don't follow. I still have a few reservations ... but assuming that it is true, it makes sense that as we mulch year after year with materials that readily decompose, like those mentioned above, the decomposing organic materials enrich the soil.

Every year, in late winter, we spread two hundred twenty five bales of pine straw over the gardens at The Blessed Earth. The big white oak, tulip poplar and other hardwood trees provide tons of leaves which are also used for mulching, and we use grass clippings. We don't catch all the clippings, but we catch the ones up near the house where we want the lawn to look nice, and spread these on the garden. We have done this for years and now we have some really nice top soil.

Last week a beautiful cat was run over and killed in front of our house. I couldn't find the owner so the burial detail became my responsibility. I got my shovel and dug a grave for the cat under one of the big trees down near the pasture fence. This is an area that Miss Beth and I haven't yet developed into gardens. I dug about three feet down and never found anything but good rich topsoil. It was easy to dig even in the dry weather we've been having lately. The leaves have been falling and decomposing under that big white oak tree for decades.

You can bet there will be a garden there by next spring. The grave of the unknown cat will be surrounded by beauty.

Prelude to *I'm Surrounded by April*

Since I've been old enough to appreciate the change in seasons, I've always been at war with myself as to whether I liked April or October best. I've often said that I'd like the year to be six months of April and six months of October, but I don't really believe that. Each of the months has its attributes, except maybe for August, I wonder about that one.

When I was a lad of eight or ten or twelve, I thought August was a wonderful month. It was one of the best months to go skinny-dipping in the big swimming hole down in the creek, but then about the time I was twelve the polio epidemic came along and many doctors thought that swimming was one way that kids might acquire the disease. No more skinny dipping in the creek except when I was sure my momma and daddy were going to town or somewhere, and would be gone a few hours.

The next essay is about how I love to be surrounded by April, and tells more about the great life Miss Beth and I have built for ourselves on The Blessed Earth Farm.

I'M SURROUNDED BY APRIL.

Written Spring 2002

For the last few days, when Miss Beth and I step outside not long after daylight each morning, to take our dogs, Spanky and Otis, for their morning romp along the stream and through the woods and pastures of The Blessed Earth Farm, I find myself singing the words to *Oh, What a Beautiful Morning* at the top of my voice.

I'm not much of a singer, but I make up for it in volume. I think Miss Beth has taken to putting in ear plugs, and Otis and Spanky look at me suspiciously and cock their heads like they're thinking I'm a little touched in the head. Maybe I am, but I'm just thinking what good fortune life has blessed me with. It's April, and I'm living the life I want to live. I celebrated my seventieth birthday this past week, and I'm still able to do most of the things I could do at thirty, although I've had to make *one or two* concessions to age.

Miss Beth often says that it sounds as though we are walking through an aviary on these bright, sun-splashed April mornings. She loves birds and recognizes the songs of most of the ones that inhabit the Upstate of South Carolina. I can't hear the birds sing anymore, in spite of the state-of-the-art hearing aids I wear, but Miss Beth identifies the species of birds by their songs. I do have a wonderful time remembering the songs from when I *could* hear them, and remembering when the April mornings were filled with birds singing their beautiful songs … instead of my woeful renditions of *Oh, What a Beautiful Morning*.

About the only other concessions—at least that I can talk about here—that I've had to make to age are walking instead of running, and working a little slower with longer, more frequent breaks. It also takes me longer to work the soreness and stiffness out of my muscles when I awake after a full day of gardening the day before. But, I consider these small prices to pay for getting to this age, and achieving the privilege of living the way I want, because I made some significant changes in my life almost twenty years ago. I'm content to let the rest of the world go merrily on its way.

These beautiful April days call for a lot of gardening. As soon as Miss Beth and I come back from our walk with Otis and Spanky we go to the garden. I've been spreading pine straw for the last few days and Miss Beth has been weeding.

All the garden paths, except one, are covered with pine straw. This is in keeping with our desire to have our gardens look as natural as possible. In the last couple of days I've spread more than one hundred-eighty big bales of pine straw, and I have about forty more to go before I finish the job.

An old garden saying is "if you don't like to weed then cover the ground with something you like." Miss Beth and I like to cover all the ground in our gardens with plants. We try not to leave room for weeds to grow.

Our gardens at The Blessed Earth Farm, however, aren't yet mature enough to shade and squeeze out all the weeds, so we still have a good amount of weeding to do. We have a lot of ornamental trees and shrubs. When these are larger they will help to shade out the weeds. Most of the trees and woody ornamentals are under planted with perennials. As the perennials mature they will also help squeeze out the weeds, but while we are waiting for the woody ornamentals to reach their full growth and the herbaceous perennials to grow to full size, we still have a lot of ground showing; and, bare ground is an invitation to weeds. We cover the bare ground with mulched leaves and pine straw to keep the weeds down and to keep the plant roots cool and damp. This mulch will also build wonderful topsoil for a few years down the road. I like to use the mulched leaves in the garden and pine straw on the paths for contrast.

Spreading more than two hundred big bales of pine straw each spring may not sound like fun to you, but it's one of the gardening activities I like best. I take my time and do a lot of other things as I go along. I keep a pair of pruning shears in my pocket and a shovel close at hand. There's always a plant that needs a little pruning, and I find a lot of little *volunteer* perennials growing in the paths. I use the shovel to move them out of harms way and into places in the garden where they'll add beauty as spring fades into summer.

Hollyhock, yarrow, sage, salvia, impatiens and coreopsis are just a few of the beautiful plants I love that spread voluntarily over the garden. Yarrow is one of my favorite perennials, and it re-seeds and spreads ... almost too well. Tall verbena is an absolute menace. I dig it up by the wheelbarrow loads. Each spring I say I'm going to ruthlessly murder each little plant of tall verbena I find, but I always end up transplanting a few to some out of the way place in the garden and then the next spring I face the invasion of the purple troublemaker all over again.

Spreading pine straw, pruning a little, pulling a weed here and there, and moving baby volunteers out of harms way is my idea of perfect activity on a day in April. Then of course, I have to sit in the sun and dream of the things that are yet to come, and do a little remembering about the hard years when life wasn't quite so sweet.

I wish April could last about six months

Prelude to *Daffodils*

Daffodils are likely the hardiest and easiest to grow flowers in the Southeast, and in many other parts of the country.

I like to take the back roads when I travel. Interstates are great if you're in a hurry, but when I travel it's for fun. I'm not in any hurry to get anywhere. As we used to say, "I ain't got no buses to catch."

DAFFODILS

Written Autumn 2001

Miss Beth and I were married on a beautiful September day in 1998. In the springtime of 2000, I took Miss Beth on a trip to Alabama to show her where I had spent my growing up years. It was early spring and although we weren't spring chickens, we were newlyweds ... in love, and in no hurry. It was one of those serendipity trips—no itinerary: just start out, follow our noses, and see what happens as time unfolds.

We visited the cemetery at *New Prospect Primitive Baptist Church* in Cleveland's Cross Roads, just outside Goodwater, Alabama, in Clay County. My parents, my grandparents, my great-grandparents and my great-great grandparents on the Hardegree side of the family are buried there. We visited *New Providence Missionary Baptist Church* about six miles north of Alexander City, Alabama, in Tallapoosa County. My grandparents and great-grandparents on the Tankersley side of the family are buried there.

I showed her my great-grandfather Tankersley's old dogtrot house, the old Hardegree home place, and a lot of other places. As we drove along the country roads, some still unpaved, I regaled her with stories of the adventures of my youth until she was probably ready to throttle me—I do like to tell stories.

But I saved the best for last—the little 88-acre farm of my maternal grandparents, Mr. Willie and Miss Emily Tankersley. This was my special place: the place where I spent all my summers from the time I was a toddler until I was about seventeen. That was about the time I began to notice girls and decided that they were more interesting than mules and coon dogs, and chasing rabbits, and shooting squirrels out of trees, and hunting 'possums until dawn on cold fall nights, with the full moon lighting my way.

All the buildings of the old home place were gone except the skeleton of the corncrib that stood stark against the soft spring sky—an Empress tree was growing up through the center of the crib and supported it to keep it from falling to the ground. The other buildings had fallen onto the ground and had begun to decompose. They would soon be part of the great scheme of the circle of life. Other trees, grasses or plants would grow using the composted lumber that seventy-five years ago was new, when Mr. Willie had proudly built all the buildings on the property.

Using the crib as a focal point I was able to find the site of the house. But it was easy to find because Miss Emily's daffodils were blooming. As a young bride she had planted them around the boulders just off the back porch.

Miss Emily's daffodils were tiny now; only about six inches tall and the blossoms were only about an inch wide because they had been in the ground without being divided and replanted for decades. But I remembered when I was a boy they had been as big as King Alfred daffodils. Miss Beth convinced me that we needed to dig some to bring back to The Blessed Earth Farm, so we got in our Big Ford Bronco and drove six miles to my brother's place to borrow a shovel.

As daffodils multiply they force the bulbs deeper and deeper into the ground. I had to trench around the clumps to get deep enough to dig the bulbs without cutting them with the shovel. We brought a large sack of bulbs back to The Blessed Earth Farm, and planted them in the gardens in back of the house. We've fertilized and divided them, and they are once again bearing the huge bright yellow blooms I remember from my youth.

Miss Beth and I now have a bit of my youth, and a bit of Miss Emily, to enjoy every spring. I can still see her coming out of the kitchen door drying her hands on her apron saying, "Winston, bring the scissors and let's cut a bouquet of daffodils for the supper table."

The next spring, after our trip to Alabama, our neighbor, Nona Neal—who lives across Green Pond Road and the big hay field, off of Switzer-Green Pond Road, up on the hill, in a house set among big oak trees—came bearing a gift of daffodil bulbs. These were also small bulbs. Nona told us that they had been in the Green Pond Community for more than a hundred years. Miss Beth and I planted them in the front garden, to keep them separate from Miss Emily's daffodils, so we wouldn't forget which was which. These bulbs too have prospered and are now growing tall foliage and bearing splendid blossoms. I like having a bit of the community—a community we have come to love, and where we expect to spend the rest of our lives—growing in our garden.

It's the time of year to start thinking about planting daffodil bulbs. Daffodils give and give, and continue to give for decades, and ask little in return. They go on blooming around old home places for generations. Maybe they are sustained by the hope that the people will come back someday and bring the laughter, and the music, and the story telling, and the disappointments, and the sorrow, and all the other emotions of families growing, and loving, and moving on to make a better world in different places, as they divide like daffodil bulbs.

Daffodils are tough little plants. They're good at keeping their lonely vigils, remembering the good times, and dreaming their dreams of hope, long after the people are gone from their lives and long after the love and the laughter have faded from the old home places. Maybe we should take lessons from the daffodils.

Prelude to *E.P. Todd Nature Center*

I always wanted to be a teacher, but I was never able to get enough education to qualify. My formal education ended when I was nineteen years old. It ended the day after I finished all my final exams in my freshman year of college. It was May 31, 1950 when the phone rang about five o'clock in the morning. It was my brother who, at sixteen years old, was still at home. He called to tell me that our dad was dead; I could tell he was in bad shape. I tried to get some information out of him about what had happened and what had been done, but he simply couldn't talk anymore and just hung up the phone. I was about thirty miles from home, without any mode of transportation.

I threw on some clothes, rushed down to the bus station, and found that there was a bus leaving in five minutes that would take me within a mile of home. It had been just a bit more than an hour since the time I was awakened by the phone, when I walked into the house. My dad was in the bed, dead from a massive heart attack. My mom was in another bed, crying like the world had ended ... and I guess she felt that her world had ended, since she was suddenly a widow at only thirty-nine. (It took her two years to get back to the point where she was able to function normally.) My brother was sitting in a chair staring into air, and my three year old baby sister was wandering around the house saying," Breakfast, I want my breakfast."

I had never experienced death before so I didn't know what I needed to do. This was in the days before 911—at least in the country; they may have had it in the city, I don't know. I called the father of a friend of mine, and he said he would call the coroner for me, and that I should call the doctor to come to take a look at my mom. This was in the days when doctors still made house calls. As it turned out, the doctor that I called was also the coroner.

So, at only nineteen, I took over as head of my family. In those days there was no discussion or even any other thoughts. I was the oldest male in the family so it was my duty to take care of the rest of my immediate family. I never did get anymore formal education after that, but I got a lot of education from the school of hard knocks.

This introduction seems to be a long way from the subject of the essay that it introduces until I tell you that one of my most satisfying activities since I quit the world of being a busy business executive, has been the work that I have been able to do as a volunteer with various arms of the world of education. I have been able to teach Master Gardening courses for the Clemson Extension Service Agency, and through this I have been given the opportunity to work with many schools which want to start gardening projects for their students. E. P. Todd was one of the most successful of these projects.

E.P. TODD NATURE CENTER
Written in 2003

Maybe the children at *E. P. Todd Elementary School* know how lucky they are to have some really great teachers in their life. I sure hope so, but it's unlikely. It took me years to realize how lucky I was to have had a few good teachers in my life. I had Miss Vinnie Lee Walker, who inspired me to love good literature, and I had Mr. B. B. Finely, who taught me to take personal responsibility for my actions—although he was unable to make a mathematician out of me.

The children at *E. P. Todd Elementary School* have Fran Grady, teacher, and Cynthia Bridges, assistant principal, and Robert W. Page, principal. One day when the students look back on their lives, they'll know, as I do now, how lucky they were to have experienced the inspiration of these dedicated teachers and educators.

Fran Grady and Cynthia Bridges and some other people made up their minds that the children of *E. P. Todd Elementary* needed a nature center. They also made up their minds that it would be one of the finest environmental teaching centers in the state. Then, they decided they would build it and dedicate it to Robert W. Page, the principal with whom they have both worked for about two and a half decades, and for whom they have a deep and abiding respect. So, they took several acres of rough woodlands behind the school and turned it into outdoor classrooms, trails, and gardens.

On Friday, April 11, 2003, Rudy Mancke, Naturalist and host of *Nature Scene* on SCETV, came to help them dedicate the *Robert W. Page Nature Center*. The most surprised person there was Robert Page, principal of *E. P. Todd Elementary School*. Grady and Bridges were able to raise the funds, solicit materials, enlist volunteer labor, and build the buildings, gardens, and trails without the man they were honoring ever finding out what they were doing.

If I listed all the people and businesses that joined them in building the *Robert W. Page Nature Center*, it would take half this book. Cynthia Bridges and Fran Grady are the co-chairs for this project. Bridges is a gentle persuader and Grady is the irresistible force that has yet to meet an immovable object. Bridges coaxes; Grady compels. They get the job done.

These two leaders enlisted aid and donations from construction companies, prominent citizens, hardware companies, garden centers and landscape architects. They called on the Boy Scouts of America (four Boy Scouts earned there Eagle Rank for work they did on the project), the Master Gardeners of the Piedmont and many other service organizations. They called on churches and *Wofford College*. Bridges coaxed and Grady compelled until all fell under their spell. *Spartanburg School District Seven* pledged their full commitment to the development of the nature center.

The trail begins at the *Carolina Fence*, a beautiful creation of stone, wood and iron. At the start of the trail is also the outdoor classroom—a "room" that has a metal roof, open sides, and lights and fans. It's fitted with picnic tables and workbenches and the work that is done there will be just like in a regular classroom, but it will be a place that makes learning fun. It takes twenty to twenty-five minutes to walk the trail, which ends at the centerpiece of the nature center, the *Cynthia P. Bridges Butterfly Garden*.

Along the trail you'll see plants as common as rabbit tobacco and as exotic as downy rattlesnake. You'll see pawpaw and Christmas fern and Japanese honeysuckle and sparkleberry. You'll see trees: redbud, Virginia pine, mocker nut hickory, dogwood, white oak and sourwood. If you're lucky you might see a deer and you'll likely see wild turkey and Canada geese. And, if you're *really* lucky you may see the great blue heron and the red-tailed hawk that sometime frequent the property.

There are raccoons, frogs, bats, turtles, salamanders, snakes, moles and birds in the *Robert W. Page Nature Center*. When you reach the end of the trail at the *Cynthia P. Bridges Butterfly Garden* you'll see—yep you guessed it—butterflies. But you'll also see bees and other pollinator insects, and birds. You'll see butterfly bushes, crape myrtle, Carolina jasmine, candytuft, hostas and one of the finest specimens of foxglove (digitalis) that I've seen south of the Mason-Dixon line. And you'll see daylilies galore. You'll see butterfly houses and bat houses. In the center of the garden is a huge gazebo that will be used for picnics and meetings.

Near the garden you'll see the *Gasoline Alley Greenhouse* that will be used to cultivate and propagate plants for the garden. Kerry Dempsey, teacher at E. P. Todd, and Master Gardener, is in charge of the greenhouse.

Many organizations and individuals have been led by the irresistible force, Fran Grady, and the gentle Cynthia Bridges to create a great nature and environmental teaching facility and a little piece of heaven on earth at *E. P. Todd Elementary School.*

The Robert W. Page Nature Center is a great lesson in what a dream and some determination can accomplish. It's a great gift to the children of E. P. Todd, Spartanburg County and South Carolina. If you go please remember to "take only pictures and leave only footprints."

Prelude to *Woody Ornamentals*

In planning a garden as in planning most projects, the first thing that must be considered is the infrastructure. At the foundation of the garden's infrastructure are woody ornamentals, which are those shrubs and trees that usually grow up to about twenty-five feet in height.

WOODY ORNAMENTALS
Written late Winter 2003

Early blooming herbaceous perennials and woody ornamentals are starting to brighten the bleak winter landscape of our gardens. Soon they'll be joined by a spring riot of color as ensuing ornamental shrubs and trees, herbaceous perennials, and annuals also begin to bloom.

Woody ornamentals are the most permanent plants in the garden and they are the infrastructure of the garden. Most of the other plants in the garden change frequently, but the woody ornamentals are usually in the same place for years. Annuals, as their name implies, are temporary and are planted for color and show. They are there for a year and then gone.

Even the herbaceous perennials are somewhat temporary. They die down each winter and come back in the spring. Many of them have to be dug and divided at least every year or two, and when divided, they are often sprinkled around other areas of the garden.

Woody ornamentals, however, are usually in the same place for years, forming the garden and being under-planted with annuals and herbaceous perennials for color and show.

I like to think of woody ornamentals as the bone structure of a woman's face, and herbaceous perennials and annuals as the make-up that emphasizes the beauty of that bone structure.

Miss Beth and I have a lot of ornamental trees planted in the gardens of The Blessed Earth Farm. We are fortunate to have enough room to plant all the plants our hearts desire, and plant we do. We've added about seventy-five woody ornamental trees and shrubs, and about a half-acre of new gardens this winter ... and we aren't finished yet.

Our favorite ornamental trees are about the same as most of the other gardeners in the Upstate: dogwood, cherry, crabapple and plum. I'll leave the ornamental pear trees to others, but we do have two Asian pear trees that give us nice white blooms in the spring and great eating pears in the summer. *(2007: with much regret we had to cut the two Asian pear trees down this past winter. Fire blight had practically taken over every limb of the trees, and we cut them down and burned them to keep it from spreading to our pecan trees and other ornamental trees. Alas, now we will only have the tasteless super-market Asian pears for our table.)*

We like to search out new cultivars of all our old favorite woody ornamentals. When gardeners think of dogwood they normally think of the *Cornus Florida* that is common to our area, but there are many cultivars of *Cornus Florida*, and many other varieties of dogwood to add interest to our gardens. There are at least two double flowering cultivars of the *Cornus Florida*: *Mary Ellen* and *Welch's Bay Beauty*.

The first double flowering dogwood I saw was in Linda McHam's garden. She has a very old double flowering dogwood that is beginning to show signs of its age. My oldest son, Mike, bought two double flowering *Cornus Florida* at Head Lea Nursery in Seneca for his home on Lake Keowee and planted them a couple of weeks ago.

Other often-overlooked dogwood varieties are the red twig and the yellow twig dogwoods. I've never been able to pin down the exact botanical name of these two plants, I think it is *Cornus Alba*, but I'm not sure. The stems of these plants turn brilliant red or yellow in the wintertime, adding a lot of beauty to a winter garden. We have one of each planted in our garden near the garden room and they never fail to garner the attention of visitors.

Flowering cherry trees will be blooming soon. A couple of varieties have bloomed already, but my two favorites, *Yoshino* and *Kwansan*, are yet to bloom. The *Yoshino* is a spreading tree, often grown in Japanese gardens for its form, yet the delicate blooms of white with just a blush of pink are outstanding. The *Kwansan* begins blooming just before the *Yoshino* stops blooming, and its trusses of blooms are fist-sized and dark pink. It is one of the few flowering cherries that bloom after the leaves appear, so the pink blooms against its dark green leaves are dramatic.

My favorite ornamental tree of all is the redbud. It adorns the woodland areas of the southeast with its bright red blooms in mid-April. Until I married Miss Beth I was of the opinion that this tree should be left in the woods rather than be brought into the garden.

When we married we were combining two large households into one small home. We requested that no wedding gifts be sent, but Miss Beth's Aunt Dorothy and Uncle Tony couldn't resist and gave us a perfect gift—a redbud tree. It turned out to be a cultivar of the common *Eastern Redbud* called *Forest Pansy*. The leaves emerge a screaming red-purple and last for several weeks, but as summer ensues, their color becomes more subdued. The form of the tree is gnarled and twisted and black against the winter sky. This tree is the quintessential woody ornamental, and has become my favorite of all the plants in our gardens.

Thank you Miss Beth for teaching me that redbud trees *do* belong in the garden, and thank you Aunt Dorothy and Uncle Tony for the wonderful gift.

Prelude to *The Queen of the Winter Garden*

I can't convince many of my friends that winter is one of the best seasons of the year. I suspect the reason for this is that I think every season of the year is the best season, except July and August. I wrote the following essay hoping to persuade them that digging a hole to plant a Camellia on a dreary looking, cold December day is more fun than laying around on the beach on a hot July Day.

The beach is okay, but lying in the sun with all that sun protection glop just isn't my idea of having fun. My family once talked me into going to the beach for two weeks. I rented one of those big old houses that could sleep the sixteen of us who were able to get away from work to make the trip. After two days I told them that the house was paid for, gave them money for food (since I had insisted that the trip would be my treat), and told them that I would see them back in Spartanburg.

THE QUEEN OF THE WINTER GARDEN

Written Winter 2000

I like winter.

I like everything about winter, except for the ice storms we tend to have here in the Upstate of South Carolina. I really like the beauty of the storms; it's the destruction they leave in their wake that I don't like. I like to sit by a dancing fire and reading, and I like sitting at the computer writing while I look out at ominous gray clouds racing across the sky.

But most of all I like to be outside surrounded by a winter day. I like the cold, gray wintry weather. I like it when the winds blow and the snow flies. I like to walk the woods and pastures of The Blessed Earth Farm on a cold winter day with Miss Beth and our dogs, Otis and Spanky. And, when it happens to snow and we can be the first to make footprints in the new snow, I feel like a little kid again. I've even been known to lie down and make snow angels: undignified for a man of my age, but lots of fun.

I like to walk when the winter rain is coming down. I like to walk when the winter fog and drizzle surround me, obliterating all but my own little world. I like to walk at dawn on bright winter mornings when the frost lays heavy on the land.

But one of the things I most like about winter is our gardens. There are practically no days during the year that I don't walk in the gardens of The Blessed Earth Farm and there are very few days during the four seasons of the year that I don't do some kind of work in the gardens.

This morning, as I walked the gardens, the sky was overcast with dark gray ominous clouds, the temperature was below freezing, and the weatherman was predicting snow for later in the day, but the gardens brightened the day and further raised my already high spirits.

The red and yellow twig dogwoods were brilliant beacons, guiding my way—the colder and darker the day the brighter the stems of this eight-foot high woody ornamental appear. The winter jasmine was in bloom: its bright yellow flowers open to the harsh elements of the winter day. Purple Hellebore blooms brightened my walk. I even found a few delicate lavender flowers open at the base of the big Rosemary plant. I miss the pansies that usually grace our gardens in winter. I made a bad decision last fall, in spite of Miss Beth's good advice. I decided I was burned out gardening for the year and I just didn't think we had it in us to plant pansies as we usually do. It was a decision made in the brilliance of the autumn sunlight that I now regret in the bleakness of January.

The queen of the winter garden, however, is the Camellia.

My good friend, Sandy Sanders, surprised me this year. He didn't give me a book, which is his usual Christmas present. The week before Christmas he brought me a Camellia—a variety that is new to me. It's called Camellia *Japonica Magnoliaeflora*. According to the tag it grows to about eight feet by eight feet, and blooms December to February with semi-double blush pink flowers. I already have a special place in the garden in mind for this beautiful plant.

Miss Beth, also surprised me with a *Daikaqura* variegated *Camellia Japonica* on Christmas Eve; it was in full bloom. This variety is also new to me. It too grows to eight feet, and blooms variegated rose pink splotched with white blossoms in October to January. I have a special place in the garden planned for it as well.

There are hundreds of varieties of Camellia. With good planning the gardener can have this orderly growing plant that blooms in all shades of pink, red, and white blooming all winter. There is also a yellow variety, but I haven't tried one yet. The *Camilla Japonica* is truly Queen of the winter garden with its glossy foliages from light greens, to mid-greens, to deep, dark greens, and even some with variegated foliage. This plant would be worth its space in the garden—just for its orderly growth and beautiful foliage—even if it didn't bloom.

There are two families of camellias; both native to Japan—*Camellia Japonica* and *Camellia Sasanqua*. The Japanese names for them are *Tsubaki* and *Sazanka*, respectively.

Japonicas are larger more orderly growing plants with larger leaves and flowers. They tend to grow naturally in tight, conical shapes and reach heights of up to 25 feet. These bloom from October to April, depending on the variety.

Sasanquas are smaller plants, usually not reaching a height of more than 10 feet, and the leaves and flowers of *Sasanquas* are smaller than the *Japonica*. Their growth pattern is loose with no particular shape—they just kinda' like to hang loose and sprawl as they wish. They bloom from September through December.

My two favorites are two very old varieties of *Camellia Japonica*, *Gigantia* and *Professor Sergeant*. *Gigantia* grows to 25 feet and produces red and white-variegated flowers from December to February. *Professor Sergeant* blooms dark red huge double blossoms from November to March.

A *Professor Sergeant*, about 14 feet tall guards the east side of our outdoor spa. After a long winter's walk or a morning's play in the winter garden, I warm-up as I luxuriate in the 103-degree water of the hot tub and enjoy the beautiful blooms, and the privacy the old *Professor Sergeant* provides if anyone happens to come for an unexpected visit. Hot tubs aren't as much fun if you have to wear swim trunks, so I drop my towel and get into the tub without any clothes—undignified for a man of my age, but lots of fun. When I was young I used to be moving so fast when I climbed out of the tub into cold winter air that it wouldn't have mattered if I'd had a screen or not. I was the flash: I moved so fast no one could have seen me. Age, however, has taken its toll and has slowed me down. I move so slowly now that I'm practically an icicle when I go through the door into the house, so I need a heap of screening.

Sitting by the fire, warming up, wrapped in a thick terry robe, with a cup of steaming hot chocolate, or if it's late enough something a bit stronger, beats the hell out of laying in the sand on a hot July day—any way you cut it.

Yep, I like winter.

Prelude to *Pansies: The Jewels of Winter*

Pansies are probably the brightest of all the winter flowers. Winter in the garden is simply not winter without the bright rich deep solid colors and the interesting variegated blooms of pansies, some of which look like little faces looking back at you.

The problem with pansies is that the time to plant them is in mid-September. I'm usually burned-out on gardening after a hard summer and I tend to sit under the shade of the white oaks, as the leaves are turning, and tell myself that one winter without pansies won't hurt. Thank goodness Miss Beth talks me into it most years. Once or twice when she has been burnt out too and we decided not to plant pansies in September, we have regretted it all winter.

Pansies can, I think, creatively be called the handmaidens of the Queen of the winter garden.

PANSIES: THE JEWELS OF WINTER

Written Winter 2000

Last night we had freezing rain. Not much, but when I went outside early this morning, much of my world was covered by a thin sheet of ice. The mailbox was coated. The branches of the needle evergreens that shield the house from prying eyes passing along the road in front of The Blessed Earth Farm were drooping under the weight of the ice. The limbs and the trunk of the big pecan tree that shades the front deck were black and shiny with ice.

The pansies that Miss Beth and I had lovingly planted in the gold and blue days of October were laying flat on the ground on this dark and gray December morning. But by noon, when the temperature has risen above freezing and the ice has melted, I know that the pansies will hold their bright little heads up with pride to cheer my day. Pansies are tough. Snow and ice can cover them, cold and wind can swivel them and blow them about, but they keep coming back for more. The gold, yellow, purple, blue, lavender, pink and white blossoms stand proud to cheer us on during the leaden days of winter.

Miss Beth and I started two new pansy beds in the front garden in October. The front is our special garden. We see it from the garden room where we spend most of our indoor time. This winter we wanted pansies there. We dug the ground deeply, added a sprinkling of triple super phosphate (0-46-0) and a liberal layer of fine ground pine bark and composted organic material. We placed the little pansies in the bed of rich soil and tamped the dirt firmly around their tender roots. We watered the plants well, gave them a thin mulch of pine straw, and they glimmered like glittering gemstones.

Two winters ago Miss Beth and I didn't plant pansies. It had been a tough gardening year and we were simply too tired to plant the pansies. We convinced one another that we wouldn't miss them for one winter, but we did miss them … we missed them terribly. It was a long winter without the yellow and blue and mauve and purple faces of the pansies to cheer us on through the long cold winter days. We won't miss planting pansies again—*it just ain't winter without them.*

Prelude to *Separated by Shadows*

Separated by Shadows is about me, trying to decide on yet another life path, after having been out of the business world for five years and on the farm for three years. I battened down the hatches on the farm in the late fall of 1993, not knowing if I would continue that life or if it was time to go on to something new. I had been living in town except for spending a few nights occasionally at the farm, but I had been spending almost all my days there.

Little did I know that it would be five years before I returned to my peaceful life on The Blessed Earth Farm. And little did I know of the major changes there would be in my life and the lives of those dear to me.

All that winter of 1993 I wrestled with the thought of leaving the farm for a while to do some other things. The question was what other things? I couldn't see myself doing the things most retiree's do of hanging a camera around my neck, putting on a pair of loud plaid shorts, and visiting every museum in existence.

First of all, during my business career I had practically lived in hotels and on airplanes. Traveling wasn't for me. And, I certainly couldn't see buying a home in Florida and lying around all day with my browned wrinkled body exposed to all eyes. That's okay for the people who can cut it, but it's not my can of worms.

As it turned out, fate stepped in—as it often does if we take our time and give it a chance. It was February and I had spent most of the winter in town; writing, reading, piddling around the small garden we had at the house there. The only thing I had found that interested me was teaching some of the Master Gardener Classes for the Clemson Extension Service. I had been doing this for three years and really enjoyed it, but it didn't take that much time. I either needed to find something to do or get back down to the farm and get busy.

If I was going to start the farm up for another year I needed to be getting about it. It was time to stick hardwood cuttings for the nursery, prune the woody ornamentals, clean the dead herbaceous plant tops off the garden, spread pine straw and about a hundred other things I could think of.

I still hadn't come up with a plan for a new endeavor. I usually have my special time from ten o'clock to eleven o'clock at night. I sit in the dark looking out at the moon and stars or the clouds and rain, have a couple of bourbons and let my mind find its own way through whatever is going on in my life at that time. I had just settled down with my first drink when the phone rang. Normally I would have let the machine answer, but it was a little late for phone calls and I thought it might be one of the children needing to talk about something.

It was my youngest child, Emily, and she did have something she wanted to talk about and get some advice on. Emily had been designing, making, and selling jewelry, as a hobby, for some time. She had decided she wanted to turn her hobby into a full-fledged business. She told me what she had in mind, and added that everyone she had talked to about it thought she was crazy to give up a good life and start over with essentially nothing. The thing was she didn't enjoy her life, although it was comfortable and reasonably secure. She did enjoy the jewelry designing, manufacturing and selling business.

She asked what I thought and I told her that I thought her friends' advice was wrong. I thought she was crazy if she didn't grab hold of the dream and try to turn it into a reality. I told her that she was thirty-one years old, and if she didn't pursue her dream, she might wake up at sixty and utter those "saddest words of tongue or pen, 'It might have been'."

Emily had a dream, not much money and no other liquid assets; I had a farm with a pretty good old house on it and was at a bit of a dead end as to what I wanted to do.

I told Emily that if she wanted to she could move into the farm house, start her business there and stay as long as she liked. Emily and her family moved to The Blessed Earth Farm in March of 1994. The years from March 1994 through September 1998 were life changing for many people I hold dear. That story will come later.

SEPARATED BY SHADOWS

Written Autumn 1995

It was my third October on The Blessed Earth Farm and the month was in its shank. I sat watching the clouds of the approaching winter race across the face of the silvery quarter moon, a moon that hung precariously in the sky, daring one of the fast moving clouds to knock it off its invisible hook. I'm never ready for October to end, and this year was no exception. My reluctance to turn loose of October was deeper than usual this year as it seemed to symbolize other endings I had been considering for some time. I had been sitting quietly all evening, studying the night sky, and trying to decide whether it was time to make some other changes in my life ... whether it might be time to take a sabbatical from farm life and The Blessed Earth Farm.

All autumn, as I had gathered the last of the crops and started preparing my little nursery to survive the coming winter, the thought had been nagging at me that it might be time to go and do some other things: maybe go in search of some new adventures and learning skills, before I got too set in my ways. Now, as I sat listening to the silence of the night, a silence broken only by the occasional hooting of the old owl down by the big spring in the hollow, I made up my mind that it was time. The old owl hooted again and it seemed kinda like he was throwing in his wisdom behind my decision, telling me that it was the right thing to do. The land wouldn't go anywhere it would still be waiting for me to come once again and turn the weeds under and plant the beans and the corn and the squash and the tomatoes and all the other good things with which it had blessed me for the last four years. The land would be there waiting for my hand on the plow to bring it to life once again.

I'd come a long way since that day six years ago when I had walked in the woods of another state and another life, during another golden autumn—that autumn I had made the decision to leave the old life of being a busy business executive, and go in search of the boy who had lost his dreams and had become lost somewhere along the way. In the years following, I had bought the farm, which I named The Blessed Earth Farm, and had established a very different life style to the one I had lived during the long young and middle years of my manhood.

As I had worked the fields and walked the pastures and woods of The Blessed Earth Farm during these last four years, the almost old man and the boy had raced across more than half a century to meet once again. The weariness was now gone from the spirit of the almost old man who was six years closer to being old; but a lot of years closer to being young. The weariness had been replaced with the freshness and the energy of the boy. The journey had been an arduous one, with surprises lurking around every bend in the trail.

I sat there in the cool evening, looking at the night sky and pondered on two questions that I wanted to answer to my satisfaction before I made the final decision to get back on the trail. I had, for the last six years, been examining my life. Could I now agree with the old sage of ancient Greece that "an unexamined life was not worth living"? The second question was, had the years at the Blessed Earth been well spent or had they been a time of dropping out?

The answer to the first question is a simple yes; I had to agree with the ancient philosopher, that *an unexamined life is not worth living*. An unexamined life leaves too many unanswered questions. Questions that perhaps *some* people can carry to the grave with them, but it wouldn't suit me if I didn't at least *try* to answer them. I sure hadn't answered all the questions that bothered me about my life, in the last six years, but I had made some progress; enough progress that I slept better at night. And I still had some time, maybe, to walk on down the trail and see if I can find more answers in a different atmosphere.

The answer to the second question, "had the six years at the farm been time well spent or had they been a time of dropping out", was also a resounding yes, they were well spent. I could answer yes to this question with about as much certainty as I have ever felt. The years of The Blessed Earth were the essential links that had brought me to my present attitude about life.

When I think of the deep satisfaction, confidence, and freshness I now find in my life, a life that spans more than six decades, and perhaps should be wilting instead of freshening; I know with certainty that whatever the future holds for the boy and me would be less without The Blessed Earth years. For, I would have been traveling the trail without the boy and the freshness of his youth, a weary almost old man slipping into the lonely years of old age.

I looked back on all my years before the time of The Blessed Earth Farm, and saw that as I moved from one part of my life to next that I built rooms of different shapes and sizes. As I built each room, I passed through it and started building the next room. The rooms were built during the good times and the bad times of my life, the times of happiness and the times of emotional and physical stress, and during all the victories and defeats that one meets in the course of more than a half century of living on the edge.

The rooms were built as I experienced success and failure, as people of value entered and left my life, as loved ones were born and as they died, as I hung desperately on the edge of the precipice, as I stood tall on top of the mountain, as I experienced sickness and wellness, as I found reality, and as I suffered delusion. As I left each room, I decided whether or not to lock the door behind me. And if I decided to lock the door it created a separate and isolated part to my life. I think that we all build rooms and lock doors, or decide to leave doors open. If we lock too many doors behind us we awaken one morning and find that we are in need of help to get our lives back together. The fewer doors we lock the more we allow a common thread to run through our consciousness and the less need we have for help or self-examination.

I had locked a lot of doors in my lifetime, perhaps more than I should have ... enough that required that I unlock doors and examine the contents of the rooms. The Blessed Earth years were the years that I unlocked the doors and went into the rooms and examined their contents item by item. I examined the treasures and the skeletons; the weaknesses and the strengths and all the other pieces of my life one by one. I looked at the monsters with fangs, and the monsters with horns, and the ones that breathed fire.

I looked at the sweet and beautiful parts of my life; I looked at the high mountain valleys with clear mountain streams running through them; I looked at all the mountains I had climbed, and I remembered all the good things that were my life. After I had finished looking at all the monsters and all the sweet things; and remembering how I had stood in victory on the mountain tops and how I had stooped in defeat in the deep valleys; and I had examined and evaluated each room in my life, I found that it was a whole life once again; an examined life that could be lived with confidence.

The hard physical work, the fresh foods, the pure waters and the serenity of rural surroundings had all helped to bring my body into top form. Unlocking the doors and searching the rooms one by one had brought the almost old man, with all his realities and delusions, face-to-face with the purity and the dreams of the boy he had once been. As they looked at each other's strengths and weaknesses, they found that they could reach compromises. Compromises that would allow them to live in harmony with the monsters and the sweet things they had found in the rooms as they had looked inside them.

The important thing they learned, however, was that the rooms were separated only by shadows and not by locked doors as they had believed. Shadows that could be penetrated at will once the determination to do so had been made.

The boy, with his dreams and magic, and the almost old man, with his realities and delusions, walked through the shadows and met in the autumn time of life. I don't know what adventures the next few years will bring. There will be adventures and learning experiences a-plenty, for the shadows have been penetrated leaving a new person living in a whole house, part almost old man and part boy. The new man-boy is now free of the bonds of the past, free to go forward, and to find new dreams and new magic lands as he climbs through the remaining years one by one.

I'll miss the soft light of the early morning sun on the rich dirt of newly plowed ground, and I'll miss the sound of the rain drops of sudden summer showers falling on the tin roof; I'll miss being able to watch the cows grazing and hear their soft lowing at dawn and twilight; I'll miss the bellow of the bull when the cows are in heat; I'll miss the crowing of the roosters at dawn; I'll miss the taste of the last of the sweet scuppernongs on bright blue October days; I'll miss the pretty blooms of the April flowers; and I'll miss so very many things of this pastoral setting upon which I have become dependant for confidence and security.

I didn't start a fall garden back in August. I guess I had already made up my mind that it was time to move on, but I guess I just wasn't ready then to face the reality of the decision ... knowing down deep that the time had come to get back on the trail. I don't know how far it is to the next stop along the way, and I don't know how long I'll be gone. I may not return next spring in time to start a summer garden, but I know that some day I will return to The Blessed Earth Farm, and I know the land will be there as it awaits my hand on the plow to bring it to life once again—as it has breathed new and fresh life into the almost old man, and provided the stage for the boy and the man to rush across the decades to meet once again—decades *separated only by shadows.*

Prelude to *Kiss me at the Gate*

I am often asked why we don't just use the common names for plants. Why do we have to memorize the Latin names of plants? I think the following essay, which is one of my favorites, will explain this pretty well.

As you get deeper into the study of horticulture you will also find that there is often much disagreement as to which Latin name should apply to a plant, but we have no need to pursue that here.

KISS ME AT THE GATE

Written Summer 2004

I rarely use the scientific names for plants when writing or lecturing for a local audience. The reason for this is that most local people in a particular locality know the same plants by the same common local names. People have grown up with these plants and have always known them by their common, everyday names. And very few people, even dedicated gardeners, know plants by their Latin names, so if I use the scientific names not many gardeners would know which plants I'm writing or lecturing about.

If I referred to one of our most beautiful small ornamental trees as a *Lagerstroemia* I would confuse many of people, but if I called this plant by its common name, crape myrtle, almost everyone would know immediately the plant I was talking about.

So, why do we have those pesky tongue-twister scientific names for plants? The answer is standardization. If I were writing for a national or for an international audience instead of a local audience, I would have no choice but to use the scientific name for the plants. The common name varies by territory, but the scientific name is almost always the same the world over.

This was vividly demonstrated to me a few days ago. I was reading *Sometimes Madness is Wisdom*, a new biography of F. Scott and Zelda Fitzgerald. The emphasis in this biography is on Zelda, who was raised in Montgomery, Alabama. Early in the book I ran across the name of a plant that I had never heard before. The author called the plant *kiss me at the gate*, and I fell in love with the name, being the romantic I am. Of course, it was immediately apparent that this is a common name and not the scientific name for the plant.

I checked all my reference books, searched the Internet, and checked the websites of Clemson and Auburn Universities without finding a plant called kiss me at the gate. By now my curiosity was really aroused, and I was frustrated. Then I remembered Ed Givhen. Ed was a couple of years behind me in high school and we had recently made contact again through one of my classmates, Jane Kern.

Ed grew up and became a physician, specializing in internal medicine, and practicing in Montgomery, Alabama. His wife Peggy is a district court judge in Montgomery. When Ed and Peggy aren't doctoring and judging they maintain formal gardens at their home in Montgomery and country gardens in country place in Safford, Alabama. They also find time to write books on gardening. I have two of their books—*Conversations with a Southern Gardener* and *Alabama Gardens Great and Small*, which they wrote with Jennifer Greer and Charlotte Hagood. The Givhens stated purpose in their gardening and writing is to find "through identification and through experimentation the plants which best succeed in the gardens of the Deep South."

I knew that if anyone could identify the plant with the common name of kiss me at the gate, it would be Ed, and so I fired off the following e-mail. "Ed, I've run up against one that has me stumped. Perhaps you can help. I've been reading a new biography on Scott and Zelda Fitzgerald. The book mentions a plant called kiss me at the gate. I have no idea whether it's a perennial, annual, vine, or woody ornamental and cannot find it in any of my references, or on the Internet. There is no description of the plant in the biography I'm reading, but from the context reference it is apparently one of the old southern plants. Do you know the plant? Winston"

Ed replied immediately, "Kiss me at the gate is south Alabama nomenclature for *lonicera Fragrantissima* or winter honeysuckle.... Actually, I love that name but have no idea as to its origin. Ed" Ed's a romantic like I am.

I think this example explains the need for scientific names to standardize our identification of plants. Had the author of *Sometimes Madness is Wisdom* called kiss me at the gate *lonicera Fragrantissima*, I would have immediately known the plant or I could have found it easily in one of my reference books or on the Internet. Also, if the author had referred to the plant as winter honeysuckle, I would have known the plant, but someone in south Alabama, would have been in the same quandary that I was when I heard the name kiss me at the gate.

Like my friend Dr. Ed Givhen, I love the name. Kiss me at the gate is certainly one of the most romantic names I've ever heard for a plant. There's nothing romantic about the scientific name, *lonicera Fragrantissima,* but the plant itself is certainly romantic. It is one of the few winter blooming woody ornamentals, and the fragrance, as the scientific name does suggest, is out of this world.

Kiss Me at the Gate is hardy from zones 4 through 8, begins blooming in January and often continues to bloom through March. The individual flowers are creamy white with an extremely fragrant lemon-scent. The individual blooms are small and insignificant, but since this plant blooms before the dark green leaves are formed, when the shrub is in full bloom it can be striking. We have a number of winter honeysuckles at The Blessed Earth Farm and when they bloom in January their flowers and fragrance certainly pull me out of the winter doldrums.

I now have another frustration. Like Ed I have no idea where the name came from and I've researched every source I can think of with no success. I guess I'll just forget about the origin of the name and enjoy the name and the plant.

Prelude to *"The Little Tree That Could"*

I love stories about people and plants that struggle against overwhelming odds. I like them even more when they struggle and win the battle. This is the story of a little redbud tree that won the battle against a big white oak tree—and me and my pruning shears.

THE LITTLE TREE THAT COULD

Written late Spring 2004

On December 5, 2003, we had one of the worst ice storms I have ever witnessed in my seventy-two years, and I've witnesses a good many ice storms. The earth around The Blessed Earth Farm looked like a war zone. We had a white oak tree brought down by the weight of the ice that was almost four feet in diameter. I've described this storm and the damage it produced earlier in this book in *Beauty and Destruction: Joy and Despair*.

Stories of struggle, persistence and miracles often come from stories of destruction. I like those stories. Here's one, however, that came from just the plain old persistence of one little redbud tree:

Once upon a time, a seed from an Eastern Redbud tree landed at the base of the big oak tree and started to grow. I don't know if the wind carried the seed to its resting place or if it was the result of a bird's digestive system. But persistently each year the little tree has started to grow, and just as persistently each year since I bought the farm in 1990, I've cut the little tree down. For the last four years since Miss Beth and I have been married cutting the tree down, however, has been against her wishes. She loves redbud trees and wanted me to let it grow. I believed that it would become an eyesore since it seemed to grow out of the base of the oak tree, and it could not get the light or the nourishment it would need because its roots were entwined with the roots of the big oak, and I knew that the oak would dominate.

Early this spring, after the destructive winter ice storm, Miss Beth lamented that it looked as though the little redbud would not come back this year, just when we kinda' needed for it to. The redbud tree was at the base of the white oak tree that split during the ice storm. But then, a couple of weeks ago, its little heart-shaped leaves began to poke above the *frost on the mountain* ground cover that grows thick around the remaining stump of the oak tree. This year I surely won't cut it down. It will be allowed to develop and Miss Beth will have her redbud tree just across the driveway from the pasture garden room, which is her favorite place for looking out over the gardens and the rolling pastureland of The Blessed Earth Farm.

Now, the roles are reversed. The little tree will dominate and be nourished by the roots of its former master as they decompose. The white oak tree will be resurrected in the little redbud tree. Perhaps even, the redbud will develop enough shade to save the beautiful frost on the mountain, a plant that requires shade in order to thrive.

Losing the big white oak tree was a blow. Its huge canopy shaded the back deck and about a quarter acre of shade garden. We've had to move ferns, hostas, Solomon's seal, blood root, trillium and many other shade plants into other areas of the shade garden in order for them to survive. We've also moved enough of the frost on the mountain ground cover so we'll have another start if the little redbud tree doesn't grow fast enough to do the job of shading it. All the shade loving plants we dug up and moved have had to be replaced with plants that love the sun.

Losing some of the big limbs of the white oak trees growing above the lower shade garden has proved to be an advantage. More light reaches the plants growing there and the plants that were not harmed by the falling limbs are thriving as never before. The plants that were damaged are making great strides toward rejuvenating themselves.

An important point to be made is that when major damage to our garden plants occurs, as it did in the winter 2002-03, it is important to give nature a chance to fix the damage before we start cutting and whacking. Some of the plants that I thought were lost forever have recovered to the point that, with a little judicious pruning, they are more attractive than they were before the damage.

Throughout my long business career, I observed over and over again that adversity presents opportunity when the adversity is approached with creative persistence. I have learned that the same rules apply in nature and in the garden.

For many years the little Eastern Redbud has persisted in sticking its head up each spring and having it cruelly chopped off. Now the little redbud is the victor.

With persistence like that it will probably grow to be the prettiest redbud tree in Spartanburg County. I know that in Miss Beth's eye it'll be the prettiest redbud to ever grow anywhere.

October 1, 2007—*The little redbud tree has had four summers to grow now and it is about fifteen feet high. It has a beautiful shape and shades enough of the frost on the mountain that it continues to be a very beautiful ground cover. The only attention the little tree has needed is a bit of pruning to keep the lower limbs away from the driveway. I won't be cutting it down again. If I did, I would face Miss Beth's wrath and Miss Beth's wrath is a force that would make the ice storm of December 5, 2003 pale by comparison.*

Prelude to *"Crape Myrtle"*

I love this little make believe story. The Crape Myrtle is by far the most popular, and perhaps the most important, tree in the Southeastern United States. There are hundreds of cultivars, and more are always being developed.

My favorite of all of them is the Natchez. You'll understand after reading this little essay.

CRAPE MYRTLE

Written Summer 2002

Once upon a time many years ago Flora, the goddess of flowers, called a convention. She not only invited her subjects, the flowers, but she called upon all the members of the plant kingdom to attend. She had determined that it was time to choose the most perfect plant in the kingdom. All the families of the flora kingdom were represented. They came from the deserts, the high alpine mountains and from all parts of the world. Thousands of plants convened at Table Rock State Park in the great state of South Carolina.

After days of feasting on the rich compost and drinking of the nectar of the clear forest streams in and around the Table Rock State Park in the Upstate of South Carolina the plants began their campaign elect the most perfect plant in the kingdom.

The mighty oak was first to speak. He rose majestically and told in a great thundering voice of all his great accomplishments, concluding with the compelling statement that the barrels in which humankind stored their most favored wines were made from his wood. The mighty oak then smugly sat down to hear the other plants plead their cases.

The tiny alpine plants of the great mountains told of their pure, clear blooms and how mankind climbed the highest mountains to search for their short-lived beauty.

One after another, all the other plants spoke. The last to speak was the crape myrtle. All the cultivars of crape myrtles had chosen an especially comely member of their family, the cultivar Natchez, to plead their case before the lofty assembly. As befitted its beauty, the Natchez was a shy, but graceful orator.

She spoke thusly, "Our family name is *lagerstroemia*. Our cultivars are many. Our years are long. We range in size from miniature to dwarf to small tree. We are beautiful all year long. In the cold times of the year our bark is colorful and our forms are graceful against the gray winter skies. In the warm time of the year we have colorful blossoms ranging from pure white to darkest red, and we bloom for one hundred to one hundred-forty days of the year. I do not say this to criticize, but most of the other shrubs and trees of the plant kingdom only bloom for thirty to forty days of the year. In the fall of the year our leaves turn all of the brilliant autumn colors: red, orange, rust and yellow.

"I don't wish it to appear as though I'm boasting, but we require little care. We grow in almost any soil, within our natural range, and require little or no fertilizer. We are very drought tolerant and require little more irrigation than nature supplies even in the driest of years. We appreciate a little light pruning if you have time, but are we are disciplined growers without pruning.

May I say in closing that we ask little, but give much?"

With that, the Natchez sat down and tucked her weeping limbs of gorgeous dark green leaves and pure white blossoms around her. A moment passed before the thunderous applause began. Once the applause had died down the proud oak spoke in his deep voice and asked that the convention unanimously elect the family *lagerstroemia* the most nearly perfect plant in the kingdom. The motion was carried and the convention was adjourned.

A few years ago I became concerned that we were overpopulating our gardens and public areas with crape myrtle. I have since realized how wrong I was; I've now come to believe that it would be impossible to have too many of these, the loveliest of small trees and shrubs, in our world.

I haven't counted the number of crape myrtles Miss Beth and I have growing at The Blessed Earth Farm. There were a few already in there when I bought the farm well over a decade and a half ago. Among the first plants I propagated were crape myrtles and many of these are now mature trees and shrubs growing in our gardens. We've also continued to collect new varieties to plant in the gardens and to propagate, until now they must number at least two score.

The cultivars of crape myrtle are almost endless. Among our favorites, growing at the farm are *Sioux, Cedar Lane Red, Carolina Beauty* and *Natchez*. A few years ago we became interested in miniatures and dwarves. We have miniatures, which are only eighteen inches tall that mound and spread to two feet across, dwarves that top out at eight feet, Sioux that soar to more than twenty five feet, and more.

We have bright red, light red, dark red, light pink, medium pink, white, lilac and maybe some colors I've missed. We were missing the old-fashioned deep purple crape myrtle, a plant I remembered from my grandmother's garden. I don't know the cultivar, but from the best determination I can make it is *Hardy Lavender*. A few weeks ago we went to visit our good friends, Jess and Allene Taylor, and as I turned into the drive, I saw a mass planting of these in glorious full bloom. I commented to Jess that their purple crape myrtles were gorgeous, and that it was a color we were missing in the gardens of The Blessed Earth Farm. Jess was my mentor in plant propagation, and, of course, he wouldn't let me leave without taking two big purple plants in three-gallon pots that he had propagated.

This is truly a plant that gives much and asks little in return.

Prelude to *Two Little Rascals*

After we lost Pepper, Miss Beth and I thought we might wait a year—or at least a few months—to get another puppy, but then we made the mistake of going by the animal shelter "just to look" and lost our hearts to the two little rascals. We still have Spanky. We lost Otis a year or so ago.

TWO LITTLE RASCALS

Written late Summer 2000

We adopted the little rascals about six weeks after Pepper, our big German shepherd, was killed. Miss Beth and I had intended to wait longer to get another dog, but one day we found ourselves near the Spartanburg Animal Shelter and I told Miss Beth we ought to just stop in and look at the puppies.

The sign on the cage of the two golden yellow puppies said they were a mix of retriever and husky, that they were fourteen weeks old, and that their names were Otis and Spanky. They were perky and friendly and immediately stole our hearts. We looked at all the other puppies, but it was an exercise in futility. Our decision had been set in concrete as soon as we saw the two golden balls of fur.

We talked to the young man that was in charge of taking care of the dogs and he told us that the two puppies were littermates and had been together since birth, but he was very vague about their history.

I looked at Miss Beth and she gave me a big warm smile, so I whipped out my credit card and we added the two little rascals to our family. We picked them up the next day at the Animal Shelter, after the vet had taken care of any future reproduction possibilities. A day later, we took them to our friend and veterinarian, Dr. Ed Davidson, for a physical examination and all the shots they needed. Then we were finally able to introduce them to their new home: The Blessed Earth Farm. After about a week, when they had healed from the surgeon's scalpel,

Miss Beth and I were able to take them to explore the streams and pastures and gardens of the farm.

The little rascals are delighted with their new home. Now, almost every morning they roam the pasture and the woods along the stream with us. At the end of the outing, we hook up their leashes and give them a little obedience training.

I'm not sure the shelter didn't pull a bit of a prank on us. I didn't study the paper work until I started to file it about two weeks after we got the puppies home, but the paper work read that Spanky was born a month earlier than Otis—if the paper work is right that must have been some long labor their momma put in. Also, they don't look like brothers. Otis is tall and lanky and looks like pure golden retriever. Spanky is short and stout and looks like yellow lab crossed with beagle and maybe a little husky and bulldog thrown in. He's a real mutt. If the people at the shelter played on our sympathies to get us to adopt two puppies instead of one, I'm glad they did for they doubled our pleasure.

Otis and Spanky may not be pure little rascals, but they are two of the most loveable little rascals I've ever met, and smart too. They're eight months old now and are real little gentlemen. They know their commands and will do them to hand signals. *Sit, lie down, stay* and *come* (sometimes ... when they aren't chasing cats or cows or birds). They know to *sit* and *stay* and let their humans go through gates and doors before they do. If cows or cats are on the other side of the gate they lean pretty far forward, but they do sit and stay until release—well most of the time anyway.

They love to play in the creek and chase grasshoppers. They jumped their first rabbit the other day—three surprised animals. They love fruit. They've been eating pears, figs, and muscadines all summer, and now that the persimmons are getting ripe and falling off the trees along the creek, they've developed a real taste for this juicy orange fall fruit. And, they like to chase cows. The big white bull ignores them, but Otis and Spanky can be real nuisances to the cows and calves.

Miss Beth calls them her little munchkins; I call them my little old dogs. Maybe we should just call them sheer pleasure.

Prelude to *Little Miracles Happen Every Day*

We were having a small holiday luncheon at our house for one of my writers groups and I wanted to come up with a little essay about the holidays. "Little Miracles..." was the result. It expresses my feelings about the holidays. I guess we're going to let things take over the world, and there will be no one left in the end to see the beautiful little miracles which take place around us everyday. They won't be able to dig out from under their pile of stuff long enough.

I can walk you around The Blessed Earth Farm any hour of any day of any year and show you a small miracle. I have a feeling of despair for most folks during the holidays. They don't even have time to recognize the big miracles much less the little ones.

LITTLE MIRACLES HAPPEN EVERY DAY

Written early December 2001

Ribbons, wreaths, and Christmas trees; Frosty, Rudolph and Santa Clause; *The Christmas Song, Winter Wonderland,* and *The Little Drummer Boy*; crowded streets and sidewalks and shoppers aisle to aisle; champagne, eggnog, spiked warm cider; *Auld Lang Syne*, a baby in diapers chasing an old man with a scythe, and firecrackers going bang, bang, bang. dancing, feasting and kissing in the New Year at midnight.

Hustling and bustling and hassled half to death, standing in long lines—got to have the latest toy craze for the kids, long lines of cars circling parking lots to find a spot to park the old flivver—tempers flaring. The next-door neighbors out did us on decorations last year—got to outdo them this year.

It's the holidays. We're rushed, angry and exhausted.

Perhaps it's time to change. Perhaps it's time to simplify the holidays. I spent the first fifty-six years of my life rushed, angry and exhausted—14 years ago I decided to simplify—simple is better.

The holidays, especially Christmas, celebrate the big miracles; the result is hurry and worry. I don't think this is what Christmas is supposed to be. Everyone seems to agree, but no one seems to have the courage to change their habits, and accept the rebukes of their friends and neighbors. It's really the little miracles that happen everyday that we should celebrate. We rush to celebrate the big miracles, which causes most people to get into hassles that give them more worry than joy. The real pleasure and joy of life is in the little miracles that take place every day: miracles that we often don't even take time to see, much less to celebrate and enjoy. These little miracles happening around us everyday will give us a world of joy if we are willing to reach out and accept them.

A new calf was born down in the pasture the other night: a few days before Christmas. Otis, one of our dogs, and I were on our early morning walk, just after dawn, and as we climbed out of the ravine that the little creek follows through our land I was surprised to see the momma cow with a newborn baby calf.

The frost lay heavy on the long pasture grass, and the black cow stood in stark contrast against the white background; the little buff colored calf almost blended into the surroundings. Mama was cleaning the wobbly new baby with her tongue as he awkwardly learned to nurse. I whispered for Otis to sit/stay and I stood watching the miracle for several minutes before the black cow saw us and moved her baby back into the brush at the edge of the woods.

Otis didn't get much attention for the rest of our walk, I was busy thinking about miracles, and Otis didn't interrupt. Dogs make good companions, they don't interrupt when you're thinking ... or maybe Otis was doing his own thinking and figured I was a good companion for not interrupting him. After all, we had both witnessed the miracle of a newborn calf being cleaned by its mama, and learning where its food came from. I can't judge that what we saw didn't have the same impact on Otis as it did on me.

This is the time of year for miracles, and as we walked the rolling pastureland, I thought about how close Otis and I were that morning to the little miracles. I felt joy right down to the toes nestled in my warm wool socks. I thought too about how we're usually too busy to notice the miracles that happen around us everyday, and how we are especially too busy during the holiday season to witness miracles: big and small.

The holidays at The Blessed Earth Farm will be fun and joyful, but we'll keep things simple. Miss Beth and I will decorate the tree, and we'll have our traditional Christmas Eve party with the kids and grandkids. We've planned a simple brunch for a few of my writer friends; we'll enjoy our gardening friends at a Master Gardener social, and we'll visit with some of our friends at Habitat for Humanity.

We'll keep our gift giving simple too, most of the money we spend will go to feed and clothe some people who aren't as lucky as we are. By giving to people who really need a little help to have a bit of Christmas, we make better use of our money, and we escape driving around the mall parking lots looking for a place to put the old clunker, and getting all frustrated fighting the crowds in the stores.

On New Year's Eve we'll walk outside to look at the stars in the night sky, and we'll look toward Spartanburg and Greenville for any fireworks flaring on the horizon. We'll try to stay awake to see in the New Year, but I doubt we'll make it, we rarely do. Witnessing miracles is kind of tiring.

Maybe early New Year's Day morning Otis and I will go walking in the pasture at dawn, maybe Miss Beth and Spanky will join us; and just maybe we'll witness another miracle. Wouldn't that be a great kick-off for 2002?

And, wouldn't it be great if we could get the world to look for the little miracles that add joy to life, and tone down the hassle and hurry of celebrating the big miracles that adds stress to life?

Prelude to *Traditions*

Traditions help hold families together. Many family traditions are built around holidays and inevitably, as the make up of the family changes, those traditions change. The change is often gradual and hardly noticed, but sometimes the changes are sudden and may cause some disruption.

I'm seventy-five years old and the traditions of our family have slowly changed over the last few years. We still have the Christmas Eve party, but it is now held at one of the children's homes instead of at our house. Our last weekend in July get together has slid off into oblivion, without many of the family members noticing. I miss it, but I think I'm the only one. With my terminal cancer there won't be many more holiday traditions—for me anyway. But I do hope the children carry on some of the traditions we have enjoyed so much down through the years.

My favorite holiday is Thanksgiving Day. When I was a boy growing up in a rural area at the foot of the great Appalachian Mountains, the family all gathered early on Thanksgiving morning at Mr. Willie and Miss Emily's house on the little farm. The Tankersley family didn't hold much with turkeys, but early on Thanksgiving morning Mr. Willie would chop the heads off two or three big fat hens. These hens were used for the stock for cornbread dressing and giblet gravy, and the meat was the center piece of the meal. My mother would never eat turkey she said it was too dry. After she started coming to our house for Thanksgiving we always cooked a big fat hen for her. (I must confess I liked the hen better too.) As soon as the hens were killed, and there was plenty of wood in the box for the cook stove, and enough wood for the two fireplaces to last the day—stacked in a spot on the porch, handy to be put on the fire as needed—and ample water was drawn from the well, and brought into the house for cooking and for washing up the cooking utensils as they were used, the men's jobs were done for the morning.

The men then got their guns and went hunting, and the women started cooking, singing hymns and gossiping. Boys twelve and older were allowed to go hunting with the men. The girls ten and over helped the women with the cooking. The younger children played knock the peg, hop scotch, hide and seek, kick the can, and many other old games that had been handed down from generation to generation of country folks for hundreds of years.

In the early afternoon the men came in from hunting and cleaned the game they had killed. A bottle of moonshine was passed around as the cleaning took place and was partaken of liberally by all the men and boys over twelve. Once the game was cleaned, it was hung in the smoke house if the weather was cool enough. But sometimes even on Thanksgiving Day, the weather was so warm that the game had to be packed in air tight boxes of salt until it was ready to be used. There was no refrigeration in that time and place.

By then Thanksgiving dinner was on the table and ready to eat. I never had to have the term groaning board defined for me. Miss Emily's table was the groaning board—it literally groaned under the weight of all the food. The men were seated and served first by the women, and then the women and children sat at the table and ate as the men retired—to the shade of the oak tree if the weather was warm, or to Mr. Willie and Miss Emily's bedroom/sitting room by the fire, if the weather was cool. They lit up cigarettes, cigars and pipes and opened another bottle to pass around as they talked about crops and mules and cows and worked up trades that, hopefully, benefited both parties.

I grew up, married, had children and moved far from the family. With no family close by, we started our own holiday traditions—one of the sudden changes in tradition. We had five children which gave us a good group to start our traditions. We had learned about turkeys and stuffing after we moved to the big city, so we had the traditional turkey stuffed with dressing: cornbread dressing. I was willing to give up many of my traditional foods to the Yankees, but not my cornbread and cornbread dressing. That oyster dressing, and all those other fancy dressings, didn't suit my taste. I had to get my momma to send me the cornmeal. I'm sure there was some cornmeal available somewhere in New York City, but I could never find it. I did get a lot of strange looks when I asked for it in stores and delis around the city.

Through the fifty years of our children growing up, marrying and having babies we built many great traditions. But change was inevitable and the time came when even the strongest tradition, our Thanksgiving tradition, had to change. A few days before Thanksgiving 2002, I received the following e-mail from my eldest son, Mike. Mike had children and grandchildren of his own, and felt that it was time for his family to start their own traditions.

Dad,

How do you decide it's time to end a 40-plus year old family tradition that is a reflection of your life and that of your parents? When is it time to begin new traditions that our 5-year old grandchildren will remember when they're my age?

My conclusion is a big "I dunno". So, we'll enjoy this year for this year, and see how we feel about all this next year, when next year rolls around.

Here's wishin' you and Miss Beth a warm and enjoyable Thanksgiving 2002.

I Love you Dad, Mike

I answered him after Thanksgiving.

Mike,

I sure hope that your Thanksgiving in the mountains turned out to be all you hoped for. I hope the food was good, the trails were smooth, the sun was shining on your bald head and the grandchildren enjoyed the nightly some-mores. We had a good time here with Betsy's and Matt's families.

As to when old traditions end and new ones begin, I guess my answer would have to be the same as yours: I dunno either, but I have some thoughts. I've spent a lot of time thinking about the subject for the last few years, since your Mom's death, and since the family has been adding generations and expanding and extending. I guess the only answer I have is that traditions die when the time is right.

I once wrote an essay, which I can't lay my hands on right now, after one of our summer gatherings. At the end I asked the question "Who'll carry on the tradition after the parents aren't here anymore?" I think I missed the point. The question should have been when will the next generations start their traditions?

One of the finest pieces of literature I know that addresses this question is the musical, Fiddler on the Roof. If you remember, it started with the song Traditions. The story is about a small Jewish community in Russia. The question is asked, what holds our community together in the face of pogroms by the Russians, and all the other adversities we face as a people and a community. The answer is "Tradition."

> At the end of the play the Russians have triumphed and broken up the little Jewish community. Each of the Jewish families is going off in different directions to start new lives, but they are saying to one another that they will always remember the old lives and community. Tradition was defeated. It seems it always is. Perhaps, that's what keeps this old world turning and forever renewing its self.
>
> But, I guess the real answer is that we will always be a family, and it really doesn't matter if and when the traditions pass and change. It is inevitable that they will do so. The only question is when.
>
> I read some guilt in your message. Because of that, I'm taking the privilege of passing on a part of your message and my reply to the other children in the family, so that they can know that, in my opinion, the passing of tradition is inevitable, and that there should be no guilt associated with the passing.
>
> We'll let the traditions live as long as they will, and let them die when their time to die comes, and no one should have any guilt. Perhaps a twinge of nostalgia would be in order, and maybe a little regret, and a whole lot of hope that the old traditions will be carried on by the new generations of the family.
>
> I love you, Dad

In the autumn of 2003 it was becoming obvious that the traditions were moving from grandpa and Miss Beth's domain to the children's, some of whom now had grandchildren. I wrote the following essay on tradition.

TRADITION

Written Autumn 2003

One of my favorite plays is *Fiddler on the Roof*. I saw it on Broadway not long after it opened; I've seen it performed on the road in various cities around the country, and have seen the movie a couple of times. I have a VHS (how quaint, but it's tradition) of the movie, which I still watch occasionally.

My favorite scene in the play is toward the end of the movie when Tevye, the patriarch of the family, is bidding his youngest daughter goodbye, as she leaves for the cold wastelands of Siberia to meet her fiancé and to face an uncertain future. This scene takes place by the railroad track as the train approaches and stops. Both father and daughter are shedding tears. The scene ends with Tevye saying, "God only knows when we will see each other again." I think it is one of the most soul-stirring scenes in all of literature.

My second favorite scene in "Fiddler" is the opening musical number: *Tradition*. It's a powerful opening about the importance that tradition played in the lives of the Jews in Eastern Europe, especially those Jews in the small villages such as Anatevka where the play is set. The villagers were constantly exposed to pogroms, and tradition was the glue that held their lives together in the face of persecution, exile and death.

Both of these scenes recount tradition. As I get older, I realize more each day the important role that traditions play in solidifying and uniting nations and families, especially during hard times.

The holiday season is fast approaching and most families, including the Hardegree family, have traditions that have lasted for years. In our family, some of these traditions were begun a half-century ago. We have held fast to the traditions of gathering at the family home, wherever it happened to be, down through the years, on Thanksgiving Day and Christmas Eve.

As the family has grown, and as the children have become mothers and fathers, and then grandmothers and grandfathers; as father and mother have become grandfather and grandmother, and then great-grandfather and great-grandmother, and as spouses have died, and divorces have taken place, and new spouses and their families have been introduced into the family, it has become apparent that these traditions must pass from the old generation to the new; and in passing changes must take place.

Great-grandmother, Martha, who helped start the traditions, died in 1997—that was the first major change to affect family traditions. Miss Beth, my wife of five years now, was the second major change, and she has accepted and has been accepted, with love, by children, grandchildren and great-grandchildren, and has become a part of the family and its traditions. As the family has added generations, those who once were children, "snug in their beds," are now grandparents and they feel a need to bring these traditions from great-grandpa and Miss Beth's home into their own homes. They feel a need to begin these gatherings in their own families.

Children who once gathered around the oven to watch the turkey brown, and who anxiously waited for Santa to come, are now grandparents and it is time for the baton to pass to their generation.

The change began last year when my oldest son, Mike, told me that his family wouldn't be at the annual Thanksgiving gathering, but wanted to begin their own gathering. He wrote me a dear and poignant note that ended with "how does one end a tradition that has lasted almost a half-century? I guess the answer is—I don't know."

I replied, "Son, I guess the only answer I have is I don't know either. But let's not look upon it as an ending: let's look upon it as a beginning." And I truly think it is a beginning. Not long after the calendar turns to 2004, I will reach my 72nd birthday and I've learned in these seven decades that there really are no endings—all endings are new beginnings.

We are beginning the season of family celebrations and traditions. Many families, like the Hardegree family, are passing the baton to new generations. Change tugs at the heartstrings of old and new generations, but as long as we remember that endings are only new beginnings, all will go well with this old world.

Oh, and one last thing—don't forget to invite the old folks as you begin the new. They like to celebrate too.

Prelude to *Independence Day 2000*

I remember when Independence Day was one of the most important holidays of the year. We had large community all-day parties. There were huge tubs of lemonade with large chunks of ice floating in them, and plank tables groaning under the weight of all the food. Politicians made long speeches, which the old men listened to and argued about later. The ladies sat in the shade and fanned and gossiped until it was time to lay out the food.

The kids had the most fun chasing each other through the woods, playing hide-in-seek and other games, or maybe it was the boys and girls of courting age who had the most fun, as they strolled in the woods and kisses were stolen or freely given.

Today the picnics are gone. The ladies are all down at Wal-Mart or at one of the other big box stores, and the men are all too busy taking naps as they pretend to watch sports on television. And, oh yes, nobody calls it Independence Day anymore—now it's called the Fourth of July.

INDEPENDENCE DAY 2000

Written Summer 2000

July 4, 1776 was a sweltering hot day at Independence Hall in Philadelphia. The debating of the language and the writing of the Declaration of Independence was finally finished. The document had been read aloud and the final phrase, "we mutually pledge to each other our lives, our fortunes, and our sacred honor" was still ringing in the sultry air of the hall.

Fifty-seven men boldly stepped forward and signed the great document and thus began the history of the United States of America, as a separate nation. A great war would be fought, costing many of the signers their lives and their fortunes, before the Declaration became a reality, but not one of the fifty-seven laid down his sacred honor. They didn't hide their identities. Their voices were raised in a loud public outcry for independence, so that England would hear. Their language was simple, plain, and eloquent, so that England would not misunderstand. Their names were boldly signed so that England would know who was responsible.

The nation set aside July 4th to be Independence Day, and we have celebrated on that date for two hundred and twenty-four years. In the years when I was growing up in the rural south, we still called the day Independence Day. I don't know when the custom changed, and we began to call Independence Day the Fourth of July, but it seems we lost something by letting Independence Day slip away from us. When the holiday was known as Independence Day we celebrated fiercely. We had picnics and the whole town came.

We pulled dew covered watermelons in the early morning and cooled them in the spring until the children's anticipation was as high as the southern temperature. We quenched our thirst with lemonade dipped from galvanized tin washtubs. The fresh squeezed lemon halves floated around in the tub along with big blocks of icehouse ice. And, we cooled our bodies by jumping in the cold swift waters of the creeks that tumbled out of the Appalachian foothills.

Brassy Sousa marches issued fourth from big bass tubas, trombones, trumpets, piccolos, and snare drums—I can still feel the patriotic chills run up and down my spine as the music throbbed through my body. Kids ran helter-skelter through the crowds chasing one another. Three legged races, foot races, knock the peg, and other active games added to the fun and confusion.

Live patriotic speeches were long and boring to kids, who were chomping at the bit to get at the watermelons and home made ice cream, but the speeches were intently listened to by adults, many of whom couldn't keep tears from streaming down their faces as they heard the speeches about the exploits and sacrifices of the men who signed the Declaration of Independence, fought the Revolution, the Civil War, World War I and World War II.

As twilight descended, string bands, fiddles, banjos, and guitars, tuned up to get the square dancing going. Young couples of courting age strolled hand in hand down to the spring in the deep woods. The day ended with a fire works display, modest by Disneyland standards, but wonderment to the kids of that day.

Today we call the holiday the Fourth of July, and most people seem to think it's a bonus shopping day to be spent at the mall in a "shop 'til you drop mode", and if they are not too tired they might stick around for the fireworks display that some malls treat them to after closing up shop for the night.

I don't hear about community picnics on Independence Day anymore and the couples of courting age go to air-conditioned theaters on the Fourth of July, and then park in their air-conditioned car after the movie to watch the mall fireworks: an isolated celebration at best.

The few parades that are still held on the Fourth of July seem impersonal, and people keep the watermelon in the fridge. Lemonade comes in bottles or in boxes of powder that have to be mixed with the chemicals we call water. It's not as good as the lemonade from the tin tubs of yesteryear, but then I read in the paper the other day that you can get poisoned by drinking lemonade from tin tubs, something to do with the interaction of the acid and the tin. I'm surprised I've made it to my three score and ten 'cause I drank it by the gallon on those hot Independence Days of the 1930s and 1940s. I even do it once and awhile today.

Where did independence and patriotism go? Where did Independence Day go?

Prelude to *Knee Deep in May*

It's Sunday morning August 12, 2007. Miss Beth is out in the garden pruning on some of the plants that think the entire garden should be theirs. She'll teach them to stay in their assigned places, or suffer her brutal surgery when they get out of line.

I wish I could be out there with her. Most gardens show the wear and tear of summer by August, and the gardens of The Blessed Earth Farm show some too, but thanks to a wonderful well I had drilled for irrigation the year I bought the farm, and to Miss Beth's dedication to keeping five sprinkler heads going twelve to fourteen hours a day, our gardens look better than most.

Our irrigation system is manual so Miss Beth has to pull a lot of hose over the two acres that make up our ornamental gardens. Pulling 250 feet of hose is one of the most strenuous jobs in the garden, but Miss Beth has done it almost every day this summer. We've had very little rain since Easter. Miss Beth and I keep wishing for a break in the heat wave, and some rain so that she can get a break from pulling hose. This week we've had five consecutive days of one hundred to one hundred-five degree heat, and no rain. The weather man tells us we're going to get a break starting today, and that for the next five days the temperature will only reach the high 90s, but there's still no rain in the forecast. Wow, some break.

The following essay "Knee Deep in May" brings to the forefront my love of gardening and digging in the soil, as do many of the essays in this book.

Not long after I was told in December of 2006 that my cancer was out of control, and that I would need to take chemotherapy and radiation treatments, I knew that most likely my gardening days were over. Miss Beth and I began to look around for a lawn and garden firm to help her with the garden. We found a good guy who works with Miss Beth. He comes for only a half day a week, but Miss Beth works several hours almost every day in the garden.

We started our search for someone to help in the garden in February, and in March we had retained Cooper Cecil. By that time I had to use a cane for walking and bending, and picking up things that weighed more that a few pounds was out of the question for me. While Miss Beth and I were showing Cooper around the gardens and pointing out the things we would like for him to do, I broke down for the first time.

It hadn't been long since the doctor told me that I was going to die in a few months or a year at the outside, that I would have to suffer the horrible side effects of chemotherapy and that I would slowly lose the use of my body as the insidious disease ate into my bones. I had suffered pain worse than I believed pain could ever be, as the doctors adjusted my pain medication. All these things had happened to me over the course of a few months and I didn't shed a tear, but when I realized that morning that I was no longer going to be able to work the gardens in which Miss Beth and I had put so much time and love over the last nine years, suddenly it was more than I could take. I guess I finally comprehended that I could no longer dig in the dirt and build and maintain gardens; perhaps it was everything coming together in my mind, as we walked the gardens which were just coming to life in the early spring time of the year. Maybe I'll just never know for sure what caused me to lose it all that morning. I felt the tears start to well up in my eyes and without a word I turned and went to the house. Miss Beth knew what was happening to me as I left her to finish showing Cooper around, and I went in the house and had a good cry for the first time.

The toughest thing for me about knowing that death is close is realizing that I'll be leaving Miss Beth alone, and yes, I've done my share of crying about that. But, that morning as we walked Cooper through the gardens was the first time that it really hit me that my physical limitations were going to keep me from gardening—my passion for as long as I can remember.

It also struck me that I would be leaving Miss Beth alone on The Blessed Earth Farm. She's a strong woman, and she's determined that she will continue to live on the farm after I die; she will continue to love and care for the animals and the gardens that we both love so much. If anyone can do it she can.

This essays expresses as well as I can my love of the land and working it.

My apologies to James Whitcomb Reilly for the play on words of the title of his beautiful poem, Knee Deep in June.

KNEE DEEP IN MAY

Written May 1999

I was knee deep in May, as I stood in the garden watching the tentative fingers of the sun poke over the horizon and begin to explore the tops of the pine trees that border the eastern boundary of The Blessed Earth Farm. I leaned on my hoe and watched the yellow fingers as they moved steadily across the fescue field that joined the copse of pines until they found me in the garden. The garden soil under my feet was still moist and soft from the spring rains, and the light May breeze complemented the gentle morning sun. I found the morning to my liking as I leaned on my hoe and watched the sun's fingers inch slowly toward me.

James Whitcomb Riley wrote about being "knee deep in June", but then he lived in Indiana. If he had lived in South Carolina I expect he would have written about being knee deep in *May*.

The morning was soft and cool. It was the kind of morning I'll think about a lot when I'm working the garden in the hot of July and August, and the cold of January and February.

I like hoeing the garden on a May morning. I like slashing the weeds out of the rich brown soil while the ground is still soft and moist from the spring rains. I like to get down on my hands and knees and wrench the weeds out of the ground one by one. I don't understand why most gardeners think weeding is work. I look upon it as a tug of war that I always win. Of course, I'm not real wild about it on a hot July day, but then there's not much weeding to be done in July if you take care to pull the weeds in May. In May, the weeds enjoy the garden about as much as I do, and they seem to out grow my perennials like a teenage boy out grows his clothes. So I get to do a lot of weeding in May.

Hoeing and pulling weeds on a pleasing day in May is a fine way to get in some good thinking time. When I'm designing and planting and pruning, I have to think about what I'm doing or I'll get my garden all out of whack. I'll put tall plants in front of short plants, or I'll plant the Irises too deep, or I'll make a lopsided bush, or make some other foolish mistake. But when I'm weeding I just kinda' put my mind out of gear, and let it idle and flit around to a lot of different subjects until it lights on one that I consider worth exploring in greater depth, then I shift into high gear and go to it.

The muses led me on this fine morning to think about how gardening is doing what needs to be done when it needs to be done. A gardener can get by with a *little* procrastination, but not much and not often. There are days that I'd rather go watch the Braves play baseball, or go for a walk in the cool woods down along the creek. But I know the garden is waiting. I know that there's fertilizing, watering, weeding, planting, dividing, digging, pruning and all the other things that need to be done in the garden. And, I know gardens don't like to wait.

Life is that way too.

We tend to put off spending time with our children and grandchildren, and our mothers and fathers, and our sisters and brothers when they, like the garden are waiting. It seems to me, that most of us are so busy pursuing *things* that often we don't spend the time we need to spend with family and friends. Family and friends don't do much about it, they either wait—sometimes until it's too late—or they go away. Or, the kids will grow up to be something we didn't want them to be, because kids, like gardens, can take a little procrastination, but not much and not often. Our children, like our gardens, just don't turn out right unless they get the proper attention at the right time in their lives.

I do go to ball games and I do walk along the creek; I go visiting friends and I like to visit other gardens, and I sometimes take a trip. But, when I'm doing these things I do a lot of thinking about my garden, and I do a lot of thinking about my kids and grandkids, who are all grown and mostly grown now. I ask myself if I gave them the right attention at the right times in their lives—they turned out pretty good, so maybe I did. But most of the credit goes to their Momma and Grandma. She was there for them all the time. They were her vocation and her avocation.

When I'm away from my garden, I also think a lot about how nice it is to reach a stage in life where I have the time to stand knee deep in May, lean on my hoe, and watch the first tentative probing fingers of the sun tickle the tops of the pine trees.

Prelude to *Winter*

Many gardeners think that winter is for sitting around the fire reading gardening magazines and studying seed catalogues. They start writing orders for seeds, and write pages and pages then spend hours, whittling the orders down to the seeds that are practical. This is okay for a few evenings each winter, but most evenings I think about what I'm going to do in the garden the next day. Sitting around the fire studying seed catalogues and reading gardening magazines is for our fellow gardeners in the great frozen north land. We could spend some of our evenings feeling a little sorry for our northern neighbors, who aren't able to garden for several months out of the year.

The experienced gardener in the south land knows that winter, except for a few harsh days, should be spent outdoors, planting woody ornamentals and perennials, and pruning and moving plants that we planted in the wrong place. I've spent many pleasant days, when the temperatures were in the high 30s and low 40s in the garden ... planting, pruning and cleaning up.

But the thing I like most about winter is just getting out and walking the land. Winter in the southeast can be the best and most productive time of year for a gardener. There's a lot going on out there ... just put on your heavy coat and go look.

WINTER

Written Winter 1998

It's winter and the sun rises a little further south each morning as it starts its circumnavigation of the earth. The sleep time of the year is here. The Blessed Earth Farm, like the rest of the world outside the bustling cities, has been wooed by the winter sandman's lullaby and is asleep. The cows find shelter out of the wind. The outdoor cats seek out warm sleeping places in the cathouse and the old red barn. The dogs spend more time nestled down in the sweet smelling cedar shavings, which Miss Beth and I have layered over the floors of the stalls they use for a giant dog house. The birds find protected places in the brush. The rabbits go to ground, and the squirrels spend the long nights in their nests high in the big white oak trees.

The plants, astilbe, wild geranium, ferns and all the others we planted last winter in our new shade garden are asleep. The evergreen trees and shrubs are fresh and green against the winter gray sky and the Christmas ferns are still wide awake and perky. When my grandchildren were young I took delight in teaching them how to identify a Christmas fern by pulling a leaf from the stem, and showing them that it looked just like a Christmas stocking. I miss those days. The grandchildren are all grown up and too sophisticated for my little tricks now.

The tops of the herbaceous perennials, in the sun garden up by the road, are dry and sere and laying on the ground, but I know the roots are sleeping in the ground just waiting for the first warm rays of the spring sun to awaken them. Some gardeners like to clean up their gardens in the fall. I like to leave the dead tops of the herbaceous perennials until late in February. My winter garden looks a bit messy because of this practice, but Miss Beth and I are about the only ones around to see it and we both kind of like the effect of the dead foliage, especially when it's poking up through a blanket of snow.

I can't quarrel with my friends who cut the dead tops of their herbaceous perennials, and clean up their gardens in the fall. They have neat gardens all winter, but a disadvantage is that the stubs of the hollow stalks fill with water and freeze in the winter, and the freeze can sometimes kill the roots. Many perennials are finicky and fickle at best, and I do detest being stood up by a daisy that I had a date with in April because its little roots froze in January.

I'm not much on sitting by the fire looking at garden catalogs in the winter. Miss Beth and I do most of our planting in the wintertime of the year. November through February are the best months to plant woody ornamentals and trees. The earth is wet and soft and it is easy to dig the nice big holes. There is usually plenty of moisture in the soil to help these plants get established so that the roots have time to begin to take hold before the hot summer days stress the plants.

In the morning we put on our warm coats and take our dogs, Spanky and Otis, for a walk down through the pasture and along the creek. Some days we see ice along the edges of the creek. Most days the trails down the banks of the ravine are treacherous with slick, icy mud. We stop often to admire the skeletal sculptures of the naked trees that have been stripped of their summer green and fall gold.

We return to the house and pour big mugs of hot black coffee and sit looking out at the sleeping world. After our coffee we go out into the winter day and begin to plant new trees and shrubs. One day soon though, we'll sit in the garden and watch as the tender shoots of the sleeping perennials peek shyly up through the rich brown earth, and we'll bask in the bright yellow daffodil blooms. We'll watch the skeletal forms of the trees grow fat with leaves and the cherry trees bloom their delicate pink blooms.

    I look forward to the change of seasons, but mostly I try to just enjoy whatever season I'm in. My view of life is a lot like that too. I look forward to each year, and the years are starting to pile up for me, but mainly I try to just enjoy the year I'm in now.

Prelude to *Miss Beth and the Tree Wisteria*

This is one of my favorites. It demonstrated how determined Miss Beth can be, and how she's right most of the time. (When she reads this, my ship is sunk.)

MISS BETH AND THE TREE WISTERIA
Written November 2003

It was two years ago this month that Miss Beth came lugging it home. It, in this case, was the worst looking wisteria plant I have ever seen, and it may have been the single worst looking plant I have ever seen that still had the courage to cling tenaciously to life. The plant was more dead than alive. The poor old wisteria plant had been in the same pot for a long time. It had been trained and pruned to grow as a tree instead of a vine.

It was a cool November Day and I was in the kitchen making a pot of vegetable soup and cornbread for supper when I happened to glance out the back door and see Miss Beth opening the back of the Bronco to take out the plant. I immediately stopped what I was doing and trotted off down to the barn to help her unload the big pot. It was a twenty-five gallon pot and should have been difficult for a strong man to lift.

I asked her why in the world she was lugging a plant like that home and what she intended to do with it—other than preside over its ultimate demise. She said I'd been talking about getting a tree wisteria for a long time, and that she had found this one abandoned in the back of a garden center and had practically stolen it from the nice man for five dollars.

I muttered under my breath that the nice man should have paid her double that to haul it away for him.

The pot was still in the back of the truck; I grabbed it firmly, gave a great heave, and nearly fell over backwards. Plants in twenty five gallon pots are normally heavy enough that I have trouble picking them up, but this wisteria was so pot-bound that the roots had completely filled the pot and there was no room for soil or water left. Dry roots don't weigh very much.

A pot-bound plant is one whose roots are growing around and around in the pot, and eventually, unless the plant is moved to larger living quarters, either to a larger pot or to the garden, the roots will fill the pot, absorbing all the soil and the plant will die. The wisteria that Miss Beth was so proud of "practically stealing from the nice man at the garden center," definitely had an extreme case of pot-"bounditus". I thought the symptoms were surely terminal.

I tried to pull the old plant out of the pot, but the roots had a death grip on the drain holes in the bottom of the pot and I finally had to cut the pot away from the plant to separate them. I looked at the dry shriveled roots and tried to persuade Miss Beth that we ought to grind the plant up and put it on the compost pile, but she was immovable in her opinion that we were going to plant it in the big perennial garden. I went up to the tractor shed and got a big number two tin washtub, filled it with water, and set the wisteria in the water to soak.

Early the next morning the plant looked a bit perkier, but I was still making my pitch for the compost pile. Miss Beth won out, as always, and we dug a big hole in the corner of the big perennial garden up by the road. I lifted the water soaked wisteria out of the tub. I took my big pocketknife and cruelly slashed and pulled the roots apart until they looked somewhat normal. We set the plant in the hole, leaving the top of the root ball about two inches above ground level, backfilled with the red clay we had dug out of the hole, tamped the dirt down lightly, watered the plant well, mulched with pine straw, picked up our shovels and walked away. I had a real sinking feeling in the pit of my stomach that we'd just wasted a good two hours work and five dollars.

The wisteria struggled all that winter to survive. We helped it all we could. The next spring it put out pretty green shoots and grew into a healthy plant. Most wisterias bloom purple. Some bloom white. Miss Beth's five-dollar bargain turned into a real bargain, however, when it bloomed pink. Pink is one of the prettiest colors of wisteria. I'm glad Miss Beth always wins those arguments.

I sometimes pull one of the lawn chairs up near Miss Beth's wisteria tree and sit there thinking about how we often give up on things—plants, people, animals, and principles too soon: like I did with the wisteria. It's nice, however, to have a real soul mate around to keep you straight.

Prelude to *Sadie's Garden and Her Secret Mix*

Most of the essays in this book are true. I took a course one time at the University of North Carolina. It was only two hours a week so I drove back and forth to Asheville to class one day a week. The course was named "Creative Non-Fiction." I signed up for the course, because it sounded right interesting. On the drive to Asheville the first day I got to thinking, what is creative non-fiction? How can non-fiction be creative? If it is fiction it is creative, but how does creative creep into non-fiction?

The thought came to me about the time I got to Asheville that creative non-fiction is not new to me but that it's what I usually write. I write stories based on real life happenings, but I take a lot of poetic license. This story though is true and I haven't taken any poetic license with it. Well maybe a little bit.

I came to the conclusion about the time I got to Asheville, and the professor confirmed it, that creative non-fiction is taking the facts and presenting them in a creative way; in other words taking a bit of poetic license.

I met Sadie and fell in love with her all in one afternoon. I don't think anyone could help but love her. I think you'll love her to once you read her story.

SADIE'S GARDEN AND HER SECRET MIX

Written Summertime 1992

There's a place in Alabama named Millerville. It's a remote place located at the intersection of County Road 148 and State Highway 9. Millerville is a little more than a *cross roads*, but not quite a village. The little farm where I did a lot of my growing up is just a piece down the road from there.

I left that part of the world when I was a very young man and moved off to places like Philadelphia, New York City, and Chicago, where I learned the business of being a busy business executive. I returned to Alabama when I was in my early forties and continued to practice my trade as a corporate executive.

As an executive I had to travel all over the country, so I spent a lot of time driving from my office in Alabama to the Atlanta airport. The shortest way was down through the country by way of Millerville. It was a pretty good road, and I don't think the highway patrol knew it was there so I could let the big old Cadillac eat up the road—busy business executives are always in a hurry.

I usually slowed to about 70 mph as I passed through Millerville, which had only a filling station and a few houses—not enough to deserve the attention of a busy business executive. But as I sped through, I would catch a glimpse of a neat two-story white house surrounded by a splash of color. I always meant to stop, but busy business executives never have time for the important things in life like a splash of color in little places like Millerville.

One day in the springtime after I had left the corporate life the previous winter, I decided I needed to go and see that neat white two-story house with the splash of color all around it. By then I had parked the big Cadillac to use on special occasions, and bought me a little Ford pickup truck for everyday use. It's a lot easier to haul garden supplies in a pickup truck than it is in a Cadillac.

That May afternoon I lay down my gardening tools, got in my little pickup, and drove over the mountain to Millerville. The time had come to find out about that splash of color. Before twilight of that day I had fallen in love with a woman and her garden.

I pulled up in front of the white house, walked up the neat rock walkway, and knocked on the door. The lady who came to the door appeared to be in her late seventies or early eighties. I told her my name and that I lived just across the mountain in the town of Sylacauga. She said her name was Sadie Johnson. Her smile showered me with peace and serenity and was in stark contrast to her physical appearance. Physically she looked like she was as tough as a pine knot. I told her about my trips through Millerville on my way to the Atlanta airport, and about how I'd always meant to stop and ask if I could see her garden, but had always been in too big of a hurry.

She told me that she had always wondered about that streak of silver that had come shooting through Millerville, usually early in the morning or late at night, gave me a little lecture on my driving, but said that if I would repent she would be delighted to show me her garden. I pointed to my little Ford pickup truck and told her that I was truly repentant. As we walked out into her garden she told me, in a quiet voice, with generations of southern lady accent behind it, a bit about her life. She told me about her early life of growing up around Millerville. She had grown up, married and lived all her life there. She knew my grandfather Hardegree, but none of his children. She had never wanted anything different.

She told me that she had been widowed for many years. She and her husband had always gardened together, and since his death she had lived in the house alone, and continued to maintain the gardens because when she was in the garden she felt close to him.

The garden was about an acre in size and she tended it throughout the four seasons of the year. The garden was her life. She worked in it almost everyday, except Sunday—she didn't believe in working on Sunday. As we walked the winding paths she told me each plant's name, and the story of how each plant had come to her garden. Her pension was small and friends had given most of the plants to her; Sadie remembered them all and relished telling me the stories of the plants, and of the friends who had given them to her.

By the time we finished our tour of the garden the sun was starting to set behind the big hickory trees, and she invited me to have tea with her in her garden. I would have preferred coffee (or really a glass of bourbon), but who can refuse tea from a beautiful eighty-two year old (she had volunteered her age) lady in her garden. I admired the way her gnarled hands delicately handled the paper-thin china as she poured.

We sat sipping our tea, and enjoying the teacakes she had baked earlier in the day, and I asked her to tell me the secret of how she grew the healthiest looking herbaceous perennials I had ever seen. She told me that she mixed her own fertilizer consisting of 1/3 10-10-10 fertilizer, 1/3 cottonseed meal, and 1/3 peat moss in a wheelbarrow and that once a year in the spring when the perennials were four or five inches tall she applied the magic mix liberally around the little plants.

I used this formula for many years and grew some grand herbaceous perennials. But we expanded the gardens of The Blessed Earth Farm to such a size that the mixing became too much of a burden, so one day I sat down and thought about the fertilizer and realized that it was really a homemade slow release fertilizer that also added humus to the soil. Realizing this I began to mulch a bit more liberally and switched to Ozmacote 14-14-14. It's not as romantic, but it does the job.

Six years ago on one of my forays to Alabama I went by Miss Sadie's place. The house was in ill repair and the gardens were overgrown. I inquired at the filling station and found out that Sadie had died and no one had stepped forward to maintain her beautiful home and garden.

More often than not gardens die with their creators. Maybe that's how it should be, but I bet the ghosts of Miss Sadie and her husband still walk the gardens in Millerville, Alabama, and I expect on their side of the curtain the house is still neat and freshly painted and the gardens are healthy and weed free.

Prelude to *Birds in the Garden*

Miss Beth loves birds, and she takes them very seriously. She knows many of them by their songs and almost all of them by sight. She is sure that they are well fed. Before we married Miss Beth lived in town where she had a small garden. She won several awards for the bird habitat she created in her garden. The Spartanburg Herald-Journal wrote a long front page article about her and her knowledge of birds. I remember one of the pictures in the article showed her climbing a ladder to fill a bird feeder.

When we married and she moved to the farm she started buying bird feeders like there would never be anymore made. She hung them from the pecan trees, the fig trees and the oak trees. She hung them from the crape myrtle, the althea and the holly bushes. She had me digging holes, and setting core poles in concrete on which she could put bird feeders.

We have three criteria, one of which must be met for any plant that goes into the garden: Is it beautiful? Is it fragrant? Will it bear berries, nuts or seeds that will feed the birds? She is particular about the mix she puts out for the birds, so she makes her own. It takes about forty pounds of feed mix to fill the feeders. In the summertime there is plenty for the birds to eat, but in the winter time, no matter how harsh the weather, you'll find Miss Beth out filling her bird feeders. There goes eighty pounds of feed each week.

BIRDS IN THE GARDEN

Written Summer 1999

It amazes me that Alfred Hitchcock could make a horror movie that casts birds as the villains. It further amazes me that the movie, *The Birds*, that Hitchcock made was as popular as it was, and that it horrified millions. I have a pretty vivid imagination, but I could never have come up with a plot that portrays what may well be the most beautiful and docile of our earthly creatures as monsters that want to rule the world. Perhaps, however, what makes a horror story is to see something gentle and familiar to us turn into something strange and violent.

Snow, ice, and sleet are predicted for tonight. That's the signal for most people to rush out to their local super market for milk and bread. But while long lines are forming at the cash registers of the super markets, Miss Beth is busy filling bird feeders. Furthermore, she usually—unless I can find a good excuse—has me busy ferrying the feeders back and forth from their hangers, which are located in strategic spots all over the garden, to the tool shed where she keeps her bird feed in galvanized garbage containers. I think she has the easiest part of the job just standing in the shed filling the feeders, while I run all over the garden trying to keep her supplied with empty feeders, and re-hanging the full feeders. But then smart people usually do wind up with the easy jobs, and the rest of us wind up doing the grunt work.

Miss Beth is very knowledgeable and particular about her bird feed, and she goes to great lengths to get the mix just right. She buys several different kinds of quality birdseed to fill her feeders. She piles her car trunk and back seat high with bags of seed and hauls them home. But when she starts to fill the feeders she makes her own magic formula mix from the several different kinds of seed she buys. She uses a cup of this and a cup of that and a cup of something else, and tailors the contents of each feeder to the kind of bird that she wants to attract. I don't understand these mixes, and that's why I'm the grunt and have to ferry the feeders back and forth while Miss Beth gets to stand in the shed, out of the cold wind, and fill the feeders.

I don't know how many feeders we have in the gardens of The Blessed Earth Farm. I have put up core poles all over the garden and attached hooks from which the bird feeders hang, and it seems there's a feeder or two hanging from every tree ... and there are lots of trees. Next time I do the ferrying I'm going to try to count them. Miss Beth told Santa Claus that she wanted more bird feeders for Christmas and he brought her a little one, a medium size one and a great big one. I thought these new feeders would replace some of the old feeders, but it seems they will be in addition to the old feeders. I guess I'll have to put up another pole or two.

Miss Beth and I also considered the birds while we were planning the gardens, and have planted many plants that produce fruit and seed to attract birds. We have lots of holly, dogwood and nandina with bright red berries. We have mahonia (Oregon grape) with purple berries. We have rugosa roses that produce huge rosehips that the birds go wild over. The other day down at George Gunter's garden center, Gunter's Gardens, Miss Beth found a nandina that has yellow leaves and bears white berries so the birds can add one more variety to their smorgasbord. And in addition to the things we plant, there are lots of wild plants and grasses in the woods and fields that produce seed for the birds. The birds at The Blessed Earth Farm are plentiful and well fed.

Sometimes, like today, when the wind is blowing and the sky is heavy with clouds, and sleet and snow are predicted, it seems a sacrifice to go out in the cold and fill the feeders. But, when I look at the black bare limbs of the big fig trees and see them full of Cardinals highlighted against the winter gray sky glowing like lights on a Christmas tree, and when I see red-headed woodpeckers hanging upside down from the feeders to reach the seed, and see a feeder covered with gold and purple finches, all of these beautiful creatures that Miss Beth attracts with her magic formula seem to make the sacrifice of an hour spent in the cold wind of January well worth while.

Besides, today I told Miss Beth I had to take care of some business that couldn't wait, and while she's outside in the cold filling the feeders, I'm sitting in my nice warm little office working away on my computer. Sometimes even dummies wind up getting out of the grunt work.

Prologue to *Abraham Smith*

His name was Abraham, but nobody called him that except his wife and then only when she was a bit upset with him. Everyone called him Abe. Occasionally someone would call him Abby, but he didn't like that and wasn't shy about letting folks know it.

I've lived a lot of places and I've had a lot of friends of all creeds, nationalities, colors, shapes and sizes, but I don't think I ever had one that I enjoyed more than Abe. We spent many hours sipping sweet tea under the shade of the big white oak trees at The Blessed Earth Farm talking the hot summer days away. If the day was in its shank, we might have a glass of bourbon instead of iced tea. We both loved to tell stories—some true, some not. When it was in the time of the day that the bourbon was flowing, the stories sometimes got pretty far out, even for us. We also spent many hours at his house, and I watched him beat one challenger after another at the game of horseshoes.

His death came suddenly in January of 1995. I still miss him almost thirteen years later.

ABRAHAM SMITH

Written late Summer 1994

As soon as I awoke that morning, I suspected that it was going to be one of my serendipity days. It was a morning too late in summer to start any major projects, and too early to do anything about getting ready for winter, except maybe to think about it.

I didn't have a plan for the day, or a thought as to what the day might bring. After a light breakfast, I got in my old Jeep, turned the key, and when the engine fired and caught on the first try, I knew for sure it was going to be a serendipity day … a day when something good was going to happen to me. I didn't know what the good would be, but I knew it was going to happen.

I put the old Jeep Wrangler in gear and eased down the driveway to the main road. The top to the Jeep disappeared years ago, but it doesn't bother me, in the summer the open vehicle is cool, and in the winter I just put on my heavy coat, cap, and gloves. If it rains that's okay too; I put on my rain jacket. I get wet sometimes, but like my mother used to tell me, I'm not in any danger of melting. It's a lot of fun when we get our occasional snow. I imagine I'm snowmobiling. The water drains out where holes have rusted through the floor board, and any pride I had in the appearance of the inside of the Jeep disappeared about the same time the top did, so I don't worry about the weather messing up its looks.

I hit the main road, got up to the old jeep's top cruising speed of about fifty miles an hour, and tooled around the countryside for a couple of hours enjoying the cool early morning air, and the gentle morning sun on my head. Around mid-morning, I stopped in the farm store to catch up on the local gossip, and maybe to buy some cabbage and collard plants to set out for the fall garden, in case I happened to get overcome by ambition, which didn't seem likely since it was still before noon and the temperature had already climbed into the low nineties.

As usual there was a group of farmers standing around the back of the store where the cash register is located and where most of the business of the store, and much of the business of the community, is conducted. I stopped up front where the plant seedlings are located and decided that it was too hot to set out young seedlings, and that I might as well put that job off a few days until the weather got a little cooler. About the time I came to this decision, a fellow in a John Deere cap walked up to me.

He introduced himself. He already knew who I was since I was relatively new to the Green Pond Community. When a new person moves into a small community everyone knows who they are almost immediately. He told me that he had been at the Farm City Day, which is sponsored by the Clemson Extension each fall. I like to play horseshoes and since I do a lot of volunteer work for Clemson Extension, they had asked me to run the horseshoe pitching contest.

He told me that he had watched me play and thought I was pretty good. He said there was a fellow, Abe Smith, in the community who was so good at horseshoes that no one had ever beaten him. Everyone was getting a little tired of Abe's bragging, so he wanted to arrange a match between Abe and me to see if I might beat Abe and put a stop to it.

I told him that I doubted I was the man for the job of beating Abe at horseshoes, but that I would like to meet him anyway. He gave me directions to Abe's house, which was just a couple of miles from my farm. I got in the old Jeep and drove down the road inundated by the feeling that my serendipity day expectation was about to be fulfilled.

When I pulled up in the dirt driveway Abe was sitting in front of the open garage in an old rocking chair, his white hair and black face glistening in the August sun. He looked at me a little suspiciously as I introduced myself, but when I told him I had come to talk about horseshoes a big ol' 'possum grin split his face, showing a mouth devoid of teeth except for a few crooked yellow stragglers.

The house was a small one story brick without any landscaping or foundation plantings. There were no trees around it for shade and the hot August sun beat down on us as we talked. I felt like I was standing in the middle of a big desert, but it didn't seem to bother Abe. After a few minutes, I suggested we move back in the shade of the open garage.

About a hundred feet in back of the house, there was a shed with just a roof, no sides. Parked under the shed was a Cadillac sporting the tall tailfins of the 1950s models. The forty year old faded blue paint had seen better days and the dents in the body resembled in number, pimples on a golf ball. I later learned from Abe that this was a trophy of eight years spent in New York City during the 1950s. Abe liked to laugh and say he took "them New Yawk folks" for enough money to come back south driving that Cadillac, "paid cash money fer it". And, after thinking for a moment he added, "And had 'nough cash lef' over to git me ten gud acres uh land, and build me 'dis house."

In all our years of friendship, Abe never did tell me what he did during those years to come by that much money. And, following my philosophy that "discretion is the better part of valor", I thought it better not to press the point too hard. I also gathered from subsequent conversations that he hadn't done much since leaving New York, except pitch horseshoes and sit in the old rocking chair in front of the garage. He must have come back to South Carolina with some money; I don't think he made that much money playing horseshoes, as good as he was at the game. I don't think they play much horseshoes in New York. I lived there eight years and never saw a horseshoe outside of Central Park.

Abe and I became good friends, and lots of days, when I was eager for one of my serendipity days, I would go down to his house. There would almost always be a horseshoe game going and after watching a few of them I knew I was outclassed in spades, and I just sat and watched.

Abe would also drop by my little farm. Sometimes I would be working in my vegetable garden and see the old blue Cadillac with its high tail fins turn down the driveway. I would lay down my hoe, meet Abe as he got out of the old car, and we would sit in the shade of the big white oak trees and talk. We talked about many things, but mostly about horseshoes. Abe never tired of talking about how great he was at the game. He was the Mohammed Ali of horseshoes, as eloquent when bragging on his horseshoe prowess, as the Mohammed Ali was when bragging on his greatness as a boxer.

I would tell Abe that he wasn't all that great, that I had seen him come close to getting beat several times.

Abe would laugh his deep rich baritone laugh and say, "Man, you jest don't onnerstand the game. I jest play gud 'nuff to beat who I'm playin'. That teases 'em, make 'em want to come back for mo'. If I'se playin' for money, dat be called hustlin', but don't play for money no mo' and 'sides don't want to embarrass mah friends by beatin 'em too bad."

We talked about other things besides horseshoes. We talked politics and farming. Since we were both getting on up in years, we talked our experiences and what we had learned from them, and we talked about family, and religion and many other subjects. We talked about our New York experiences, but not about how Abe came by his money. Abe proved to be loquacious on all subjects, and I've never been shy when it comes to talking and telling stories so our friendship ripened. We were just an old black man and an old white man who grew up about the same way, but whose adult lives had been as different as the color of our skins, sitting in the shade swapping stories. Some true, some perhaps falling into the realm of our imaginations. One autumn several years later, on a high blue October day, I once again ran the horseshoe pitching contest at the Farm City Day Celebration.

The rule was that a winner took on all comers until he, or she, was beat in a game of twenty-one points. I asked Abe to come and start the game with any opponent that showed up. He accepted with relish—the big ol' 'possum grin splitting his face into a picture of pure delight. He said, "Man, I be there bright and early, but you know once I git up, I be up the rest of the day. Ain't nobody gone sit ol' Abe down"

He came that bright blue, warm, golden day in early October; he took on all comers putting them down one by one all morning. I noticed up in the morning that he was wincing when he bent over to pick up the shoes, and went over and asked him about it.

He said, "Got a little pain in my belly, ain't notin' to worry 'bout."

When lunch time came, Abe was still king of the mountain. I went over to him between games and asked him to come let me buy him a lunch. He hadn't taken a break all morning. He had stood and pitched those heavy horseshoes hour after hour, and as he bent over to pick up the horseshoes, I noticed that the grimace of pain on his face was becoming more pronounced.

Abby said, "I think maybe I pass up lunch. I druther play than eat, 'sides I ain't hungry."

I couldn't convince him to stop and eat, so I went over to the tent where the men from the Methodist Church were selling sandwiches and had a couple of hot dogs. After I'd eaten I ambled back over to the horseshoe pitching range and Abe was still beating everybody that challenged him. He sat them down one after another. The news of Abe's skill at pitching horseshoes spread and the line waiting to take him on was longer than it had been all day.

When the party was over, and the fairgrounds were ready to close at four o'clock, Abe was still playing. He had been on his feet throwing the heavy horseshoes for seven hours, and in spite of the pain which had worsened as the day lapsed, he hadn't lost a game.

As we left that Saturday afternoon he told me that this had been one of the best days of his life. That from now on everyone was going to know that he was the best horseshoe player in Spartanburg County.

I asked him about his pain and he told me that on Monday morning he was going into the hospital for some tests. I wished him luck and told him to call me as soon as he had any results. We agreed that there couldn't be anything seriously wrong with him, the way old men do when they're like boys whistling as they walk through the graveyard at midnight.

When I hadn't heard from Abe by Wednesday, two days after the tests, I called his home. The rich baritone didn't have the joy in it that night, and I could tell the news was not good. "Man, tey tink maybe I got cancer. Gon' let me know fer sure on Friday."

My friend Abe died about three months later. The cancer was too far gone to even consider treatment.

I miss my old friend. I miss seeing the old Cadillac turn off the blacktop road and come down my driveway. The old car still sits under the open shed in Abe's back yard, the faded paint blue against the green weeds growing up around it. The weeds have almost reached the windows now; I guess eventually the Kudzu will come and claim the old Cadillac.

I miss hearing Abe brag in his rich laughing baritone voice as we sit under the big white oak trees, drinking iced tea, and talking the day away. I miss his snaggled tooth 'possum grin, and the twinkle in his almost black eyes as he tells his stories of "New Yawk" and how he—"tuk dem Yankees fer 'nuff money to git me a new Cad'lac car, and ten gud acres, and build me a brick house, and live purty gud widout workin'. 'Lows mo' time fer hoss shoes."

I know somewhere old Abe is laughing, and taking on all comers and winning, and bragging.

It's okay for Abe to brag: he earned his bragging rights.

Prelude to *Harmony of Change*

All through life we talk about change and it has become an axiom by now that 'the only thing that is certain in life is change.' Those of us who garden or who spend a good deal of our time in the out of doors can probably better attest to the fact that things are always in a state of change, than any other group of people.

We see the subtle change. Many of my friends who go outside as little as possible often say things like we just didn't have any spring this year, it jumped from winter right into summer. The change was there. It may not have been dramatic as it sometimes is, and because of that my friends who spend their time glued to their desks at work and their television sets at home just didn't notice the change because it was so subtle.

Those of us, whose daily activities are outdoors, notice the change. We notice also that the change brought about by nature is almost always in harmony; whereas the change brought about by man is often in conflict. I believe that Man will one day begin to strive for the harmony of change that is found in the natural world, instead of the conflict of change that is often brought about when Man directs the change.

I wrote the following essay during one of those years when the change from winter to summer had not been dramatic, and indoor people were walking around, wiping sweat from their foreheads, saying, "we just didn't have any spring this year, it jumped from winter cold directly into summer hot." The spring was there, but it was subtle enough and in such great harmony that the indoor people failed to notice it.

THE HARMONY OF CHANGE

Written Summer 2003

Gardens change. They change hour by hour, day by day, month by month, and season by season. The puppies, Otis and Spanky, and Miss Beth, and I walk the gardens, pastures and woods of The Blessed Earth Farm most mornings of the year. We walk on cold windy winter mornings, and on summer mornings when the heat comes up with the sun. We walk in the soft rain of spring mornings, and in the golden warmth of autumn mornings. We like to see the change.

March is often a month of dramatic change, an especially good time to walk the land. The big sun garden up by the road starts to awaken in February, and by March it's a bustling riot of change: there's a lot going on. The most hardy and daring bulbs, daffodils, crocus, and hyacinths, began to poke their heads into the frigid air of February, and by March they are in full bloom. Daylilies are fresh and green and Iris rhizomes send up fresh green sword shaped leaves.

March brings my favorite of all the plants, the woody ornamentals, to life. Pussy willows show their fluffy white blooms. Kiss me by the gate is just finishing its season, but the delightful fragrance that has blessed the garden most of the winter still lingers to enhance the early March beauty of Okame cherry trees, whose bright pink cones of cotton candy light up the garden on dreary March days. Pale pink Yoshina Cherry and deep pink Kwanzan Cherry are waiting in the wings to bring forth their glorious beauty as March begins to wane. Forsythia shines bright gold in the morning sun. White and red flowering quince sparkle like diamonds and rubies. Fuchsia colored redbud trees jolt the eye. The flower buds of rhododendron, like a woman nine months pregnant, are full to bursting, and the leaf buds are lurking in groups of three or five beneath the buds to put on new growth once the blooms have finished.

In Miss Beth's pasture fence garden the lilac buds look like galls up and down the length, and on the tips of the branches. Hostas, astilbe, and the bleeding hearts are beginning their growth into spring. Silver gray leaves of butterfly bush add an understated beauty to the garden and the new lime green shoots of Autumn Joy sedum stand bright against the dark soil.

The shade garden is the last of the gardens to awaken as the spring equinox approaches, but the dark purple, lime green, lavender, and white blooms of the hellebores are marbled with dark mauve spots that add to their interest and beauty. They have been blooming since December brightening the long days of winter. The climbing hydrangea that we planted to climb the trunk of a little white oak tree has flower buds that rival the shape of a pot-bellied pig, and the Carolina Jasmine, which we planted to crawl along the trunk of the big poplar tree that was felled in an ice storm a couple of years ago, is starting to show color.

Otis and Spanky always forget their manners and start straining at their leashes as we approach the big pasture. They know their time to romp has come. It's their time to bark at the cows and to chase hundreds of robins that are walking the greening fescue, looking for early morning worms that have been chased above ground by the spring rains. We command them to sit as we open the pasture gate and unhook their leashes. They sit leaning anxiously forward, and on the command of *okay go*, they shoot like bullets out of the muzzle of a gun and are over the first hill before Miss Beth and I can close the gate.

The dogs roam at will as we meander along the creek. The red leaves of the swamp maple are half grown already, and the buds on the native azalea are almost open. Hickory, persimmon, tulip, and white oak tree leaf buds are starting to puff open. The water in the creek runs clear and bright and we see little fishes swimming in the deeper pools. We are blessed with a maintenance free water garden. Otis and Spanky visit for a treat or a pat on the chest, and are gone again to find a rabbit to chase into a briar patch or a squirrel to chase up a tree.

Life is good in the gardens of The Blessed Earth Farm. Our world of nature is in the *harmony of change*.

Prelude to *The Alter of Change*

Changing habits which were formed over almost four decades comes slowly. It took a long time for me to get used to getting up in the morning putting on jeans and a tee shirt, as opposed to a Brooks Brother's business outfit. It took time to get accustomed to climbing up in the big Ford Bronco and going to The Blessed Earth Farm instead of stepping down into the shinny Cadillac and going to the office. I was truly in a state of metamorphosis. A metamorphosis that moved very slowly, but each day I became a little more comfortable that what I was doing was the right thing, and that it was bringing me to that state of peace and contentment in life.

Strangely, after I quit the world of business, I had nightmares over money. I had determined that I had enough money to last me for the balance of a long life if I invested and managed it wisely, but several times each month I would wake up in the middle of the night, sit straight up in bed and say in a loud voice, "I've got to get out of this damn bed and go and find a job. I've got to earn a living." My wife would wake me, and tell me that I had told her that we had enough money to last us for our lives. I would reassure her that this was true, and sometimes that took a while because she didn't understand investing money and the magic of compound interest, and all those other good things that can happen when you invest wisely. Sometimes we both lost a good part of a nights sleep because of one of my nightmares, however erroneous.

It was hard to get used to not working for money. I had worked for money and had never had to take a penny from anyone since I was twelve years old. Although these night time episodes became less frequent it took me almost ten years to get over them entirely.

THE ALTAR OF CHANGE

Written Summertime 1997

The Blessed Earth was *my* "promised land". It was the altar of change; the place where the metamorphosis began. Here I found the atmosphere to begin my change from the busy business executive to the seeker of lost dreams. It is a difficult task to go back more than five and a half decades in time, and try to recapture growing up years and to mesh them into the character that had become the almost old man. *(2007: I used almost old man, because this was written in 1997, when I was only sixty-five years old. All you young 'uns stop laughing sixty-five isn't old when you get there.)* And, it is nigh on to impossible to take the young man and adapt him to the almost old man. But the real problem was in taking the years of *the man* and gearing them to mesh smoothly with the mechanism of the boy, the young man, and the almost old man.

The boy had believed in magic, and the young man had gone forward, full of dreams and idealism. But *the man* had trod the world for years in pursuit of worldly success, making sure that he accumulated enough trade goods—houses, clothes, cars, the right schools, the right neighbors and neighborhoods, the right country clubs—and all the other right things which must be acquired in order to be a success in the eyes of the corporate world. The man had run the gauntlet thrown down by competition, had risked all on the outcome, and was inclined to influence the outcome by whatever measures necessary. The man had been too busy to take care of the things he thought were deserving of higher priority in his life. The battle had left emotional scars in abundance.

Somewhere back near the beginning, when the young man was starting out, and when he first began to make compromises with his dreams, the melody and the words of his song began to separate, and as the years passed they turned more and more away from one another, until they could no longer see each other as they traveled to their separate valleys—a high mountain in between. Now, the almost old man's task was to take all these roles of days past and tune them into a single melody that could live the balance of his years with joy and satisfaction. The old man had a truly Herculean task in front of him.

The farm is a blessed place. It provided the opportunity for the hard physical work needed to tune the body, and it offered the solitude for the pondering and remembering needed to tune the mind and the spirit. It is located in a community that is cut from pure heart pine. There is no place for plastics in this world.

The people of the community are simple in their beliefs, and principled in their ways. They have had their own healing effects on the conglomeration of forces working to make an almost old man whole again. They have no awe of rank or wealth. They hold no wonderment for social position or office. They expect people to be honest, as defined by the old standards; they expect people to help their neighbors and to be kind to those who are less fortunate or weaker, and they have little patience for a play on semantics: in their dictionary these terms are unequivocal, and not in need of further definition. These were their rules for acceptance into their community, and into their lives. I came to this place and found it healing.

Once in a while someone asks me if I miss the old life, the one of the power and luxury and money, and my answer is an unequivocal *no*.

I worked the fields of The Blessed Earth in the cold of winter and in the heat of the noon July sun. I sat and shelled butterbeans and shucked sweet golden corn in the shade of the big white oak trees. I rested beside the still waters of the big spring down in the hollow. I walked the pastures in the snows of winter and I roamed the woods in the gold of autumn. I sat at night in the openness, and watched the night sky, and saw the moon in all its phases. I learned once again the names of the constellations—names the boy knew, but that the man had forgotten somewhere along the way. I watched the approaching clouds of winter as they chased each other across the face of the full moon. I listened to the bellowing of the rutting bull, and I watched calves being dropped in the spring when the grass was greening.

I grew long slender green beans, deformed looking yellow squash, cylindrical dark green cucumbers, round purple eggplants, yellow bullet ears of corn, butterbeans fat and speckled, and big yellow pumpkins. I grew all these and more. And when they were full to bursting, and ready for harvest, I gathered them to me from the fertile fields, and then I shelled them and snapped them, and shucked them, and cut them into pieces, and all the other things you have to do to them to preserve them, and then on the cold gray days of winter I tasted the summer sun.

On hot July days, I picked bushels of figs from the fig trees that an old woman had planted in years long gone by. I picked blackberries from the brambles that grew wild along the creek, made by the waters of the big spring in the hollow. I picked strawberries and blueberries from the vines and bushes I had planted last summer and the summer before. Then, I made them all into preserves to go on hot buttered biscuits on cold winter mornings; and, except for the figs, I put them into an old hand-cranked ice cream freezer I found in the old barn, with milk and eggs and rich heavy cream and sugar, and turned them into ice cream, which helped make the hottest of July days a little more bearable.

I picked muscadines and scuppernongs on high blue, warm September days and ate the grapes and made juice from them. I picked up pecans from under the big pecan trees on cold blustery days in November and made pies, and toasted and chopped them to put in buttery mashed sweet potatoes for my Thanksgiving dinner.

I went to the garden on long cold days in January and pulled the green leaves of lettuce for a taste of spring freshness on my winter table, and I cut cabbages so big I had to haul them from the garden one by one. In December, I cut broccoli the color of the winter sea; in January, I cut snow white cauliflower. I dug big orange sweet potatoes from the winter mounds of pine straw and dirt where I had stored them, and I baked them and made them into pies and I gloried in their sweet nourishment.

I did all these things and more, and as I did them I remembered the things that have been, and pondered the things that are, and hoped for good things of joy to come.

And as I remembered, and pondered, and hoped, the healing of the body and spirit, and the uniting of the forces that were to be the new man were happening little by little.

Prelude to *Time*

This is the last essay in the book. I wrote this essay almost ten years ago when I felt I was king of the world. I had quit the world of the busy business executive ten years before. I was living by the calendar and the seasons, and I felt that I was well on the way to reaching the goal I had set for myself.

Now, twenty years after leaving the corporate world I feel that I have reached that goal: to be happy, content and at peace most of the time.

Time, however, has conquered all. I know that within a few months my body will no longer be able to fight the good fight that it has fought for the last eleven years and the cancer will win the last battle.

TIME

Written Summer 1998

I walked slowly out across the watermelon patch in the South Carolina July afternoon heat. I wanted a watermelon for supper, and hadn't thought to pull one in the cool of the morning. I thought about the melon while I was having my lunch, under the cool shade of the big trees up behind the house, and now I was paying for the mistake of not pulling it earlier by having to go into the field in the afternoon heat. The melon would be cool in time for supper if I soon got it floating in the fifty five degree water of the big spring down in the hollow.

Like most people and other living things that live in the deep south, I try to avoid going out into the fields when the temperature pushes the mercury over hundred degrees, as it had this early July afternoon. As far as I could see, I was the only thing moving around in the heat. It seemed like the world had suddenly been depopulated, leaving me alone in a white hot wilderness. The cows had gone to ground and were standing belly deep in the cool waters of the creek that ran along the west side of the farm property. They were relishing the shade of the tall tulip trees that had been growing along the creek banks since the Indians roamed the land of The Blessed Earth Farm. Keeping cool was more important to the cows than eating, which is usually a full time occupation with them. The squirrels and birds had disappeared into their nests high in the trees and low in the brush. The rabbits and chipmunks had long ago sought the coolness of their underground warrens. Honey bees have enough sense to do their work in the cool temperatures of the early morning and the late afternoon; even the bumble bees and the carpenter bees, which can usually be seen flying lazily along on the hottest day, were taking a siesta this day, one of the hottest days on record.

It was an afternoon to take things slow and easy, not to make any sudden moves or get into any kind of rush, if you had to move around at all. But I could already taste that watermelon for supper, so I walked slowly through the heat of a world that was hushed and still. Once in a while I could hear a car or a truck go by up on the main road, but the people traveling in them didn't count as being alive in my world, for I knew they were riding along in their cocoon of cool air with their windows closed, insulating them from the real world of heat and sun and stillness; they might as well have been on another planet.

As I moved through the quiet hot stillness it seemed that even time was suspended. With a little imagination I could have convinced myself that I had stepped into H.G. Wells' time machine and pushed the stop button.

Alone in a world where time had stopped, I got to thinking about an article I had read in the local newspaper a few days before. I could tell that the fellow who wrote the article was a consultant. Back when I was a busy business executive I used to deal with a lot of consultants, and I had read a lot of the same kind of articles as this one I saw in the paper. When I was in business I hung on every word they said, and even paid them well for their advice. The article was written by a fellow who had a lot of letters behind his name, and called himself a *time expert*. He told all about how, if we want to be successful, we have to plan every minute of our day. He talked about how we had to look back at the time we had wasted in the past, and try to figure out ways to better use time to take care of more profitable things in the future. He said that we had to look at our future schedules to be sure we were using every minute to take care of the details of our business. I guess he was a smart man, as all his degrees claimed him to be, but standing there in my own little world, with time stopped, I began to suspicion that he might need to stop and reconsider some of his thinking.

I watch people rush around, trying to do more than they can in a day, scurrying to and fro trying to take care of all the details of their busy lives, and in the process adding more details to be taken care of. I remember not so long ago, that was the way I did things too. I read the articles about stress and what it's doing to people: its effects are making them everything from a little bit sick to totally incapacitated. Reports of how moms and dads are abusing their children and blaming it on stress; how spouses are beating up on one another and blaming it on stress too; how people are going berserk, picking up assault rifles and killing people, and blaming it on stress; how not having a good job that provides the money to have everything they want is causing stress because people are working two jobs—or sometimes four jobs between husband and wife. There was a couple on the news, just the other day, who had five jobs between them, no children, and still, they couldn't get by on what they were earning. I think about all the experts telling them how to arrange their schedule so that they can do even more, and I wonder if we shouldn't consider some alternate ways to go about this thing—*life*. It seems to me that we have a major kind of problem when we are so busy chasing money that we don't have time to take care of the important things in our lives.

I moved on to thinking about how time, counted in seconds, is so important to people today, but how time, counted in hours or even days, didn't make much difference to people in the simpler days back ten or twelve decades ago; a time when people were happier and better satisfied. If I can believe what I read and trust what the old folks tell me, it was a time when folks hadn't yet been programmed to want so much; a time when folks didn't know that there was such a word as stress, or if they did, it applied to the stress load of steel or concrete, not to the stress load of people.

People tell me they have to count the seconds of their day, and make every one count if they are going to keep up. It puzzles me what they are keeping up with. When I ask them they look kind of blank, and after a few moments they say something like—you know—I have to keep up with the bills, with my needs, with the children's needs, you know.

Think about it, you're chasing more money to try to keep up with paying the bills, when simply cutting out most of the *wants* of you and your children, and focusing on *needs*, would provide freedom from the extra time and stress of trying to make more and more money. Half the money you spend, after all, is likely going to pay for unnecessary *wants*. Start asking yourself before you buy things, "Do I need this? Is it really worth what I have to do to have it?" We could all be happier, I guarantee it.

Children don't need ten speed racing bikes, expensive video games, athletic shoes that cost a half-week's pay for the average person, more clothes than they can get around to wearing before they out grow them, and all the other *things* that the advertising companies on Madison Avenue have convinced them to beg for until you become convinced that they need these things. Then suddenly, a *want* erroneously becomes a *need*. The answer is not to go chasing more money, but to cut the *wants* down to *needs*. Some of the pay check, from just one job may even be left over at the end of the month. You can begin putting money into the bank, instead of piling up credit card debt.

Children need simple nourishing food, clean clothing that is comfortable and reasonably presentable, warm shelter, time to play and have fun, and they need parents who have time to spend with them and to love them. Beyond this, they only need a chance at whatever level of education they are capable of achieving, which doesn't have to cost a lot of money—there are scholarships, and low interest loans that go wanting, because people don't take time to look for them.

Nor do you adults need all the things Madison Avenue has convinced you that you need; like fifty thousand-dollar cars, five thousand square foot houses that cost more that you can afford, a different wardrobe for every day, and the many other expensive *things* that it would take three extra pages to name. You need the same things children need, and you need a way to earn enough money to supply these simple needs, hopefully in a job that you enjoy and that will permit you the *time* to provide the love that your children want and *so badly need*.

You especially need the time to have fun with your children, and to teach them what's right and wrong, and maybe a few manners. Henry David Thoreau wrote in *Walden*, "Our life is frittered away by detail. An honest man has hardly needs to count more than his ten fingers, or in extreme cases he may add his ten toes, and lump the rest. Simplicity! Simplicity! Simplicity! I say let your affairs be as two or three and not as a hundred or a thousand."

Other people have expressed this thought down through the ages, but I think Henry said it best. I'm not going to try to improve on it. I just want to say that it came back to me on a searing hot afternoon in a watermelon patch; an afternoon when time wasn't important, because time stood still in my world. I think the message bears repeating today.

We need to prune our affairs and our wants just as surely as we need to prune a favorite shrub. It is difficult to take pruning shears in hand and prune away the excess growth that has come about because you wanted more for your shrub. It is even more difficult to prune your affairs that were born of a desire to give your children more. It is easier if we remember that a child, like a shrub, will grow up healthier if we give it the attention and love it needs, which in both cases requires consistent *pruning*.

Maybe it's time for us as a country to look at what we are doing to ourselves, and to try to get our wants and affairs in order. Maybe it's time for us to look at some of the things that are important, like spending time with our kids and loving them, and teaching them about the good things in life, instead of trying to give them, and ourselves, everything we see advertised.

Maybe it's time for us to spend a little time in a place where time stands still, like a watermelon patch on a hot southern afternoon, or sitting in the shade of white oak trees listening to the big spring gurgle out of the ground, or walking the banks of a creek looking for mud turtles. Maybe it's time for us to sit out under the stars and look at the night sky and introduce ourselves to the man in the moon again. Maybe it's time we did these things with our children, and in doing things with them, to help them to see what's really important during our years here on this beautiful green planet.

One thing we must recognize as paramount is that we don't own time. Time has the first word in our lives, it will have the last word in our lives, and it will have the most to say in between.

I do agree with the *time experts,* that time is precious and must be used wisely. Where we disagree is in defining the meaning of *wisely.* The experts believe that time must be managed to take advantage of each minute for conducting our affairs. I believe that we must manage the time we have been given, the time which we call our lives, to squeeze in as many of the truly important things as possible: the joy of being with our children and grandchildren, and with family and friends; the joy of learning; the joy found in great books and music and plays; the joy of walking a dirt road in the freshness of the early morning, and in resting in the weariness of the evening. We only have one chance. What a pity it will be if we find ourselves crying out on our death bed, "I can't die now, I haven't lived yet."

Maybe it's time we got back to being good to ourselves

Epilogue

Written October 2007

It's five o'clock in the morning and I awakened about 20 minutes ago. Each morning it's getting more difficult to get out of bed. Each day I get a bit weaker and each morning my body hurts more and my bones and muscles are stiffer. It's almost impossible to force my body to start the process of getting up, but staying in the bed is not an option. Because of pain in the various parts of my body I can only sleep in one position and even though it's a bit early that position is used up for this night.

I reach over and pick up my walking cane. Using it for leverage, I'm finally able to sit up and then using it for balance I am able to stand. Those first steps are excruciating. It seems pain is everywhere. The legs almost refuse to obey the command of the brain to move. And the brain realizes that it can't push too hard: balance must be taken into consideration. A fall resulting in a broken bone at this time would be tragic. Most likely the bone would never mend and this might leave me in bed for the rest of my life.

Once I'm moving things become easier and I reach for my clothes and start the slow process of getting dressed. I struggle to put on my underwear, pants and shirt. I'm thankful that the morning is warm and I won't have to put on shoes and socks. Reaching my feet to put on socks and then shoes is becoming beyond challenging, but on those mornings when the weather is cool I strain through the pain until I have it done. There's not much circulation in my lower legs and feet anymore and shoes and socks are necessary to keep my feet warm if the house is the least bit cool.

I know that soon I'll need help with the simple task of putting on my shoes and socks. Something I've done since I was a small child, but in a few weeks will no longer be able to do by myself. Last week I had to ask Miss Beth to trim my toenails. She does this cheerfully, and I know the cheerful feeling is sincere on her part, but still it is humbling to me. As she finishes she looks up and sees that my eyes are glistening with tears. She knows what I'm thinking and her big beautiful eyes begin to mist. She says, "You know I'm glad to do this." I say that I know she is, but that it's one more thing that I couldn't do for myself. One more way this insidious disease humbles one. We didn't have to say anything more for we both know that there will be bigger humbling experiences down the road. When that time comes, I know Miss Beth will be more than willing to handle these matters for me, but I know that it won't be easy for her and I know how hard it's going to be on my ego.

To not be able to do these simple physical tasks is almost more than I can bear at times. After all I'm the guy that until he was sixty-five years old, jumped out of bed at five o'clock in the morning and ran five miles shouting with joy in the rain, wind and snow, and shouted with even more joy on those beautiful cool fall mornings. I'm the guy who backpacked more than half of the Appalachian Trail. I'm the guy that at seventy could out-work most much younger guys. Now I'm the guy who can't trim his toenails and will soon go through even more humbling experiences, though once he could walk up steep mountain trails with a fifty-pound pack on his back.

I walk to the kitchen and put on a pot of coffee. I've moved around enough by now to realize that not all the pain is caused by being immobile during the night, that part of it is caused by the cancer, especially the pain in my spine and pelvic area. It's still almost two hours until time for my regular morphine dosage, which is in pill form. I am, however, permitted a certain amount of morphine daily in liquid form when the pain flares up. The liquid is much quicker acting. I reach for the bottle and carefully measure thirty milligrams into about an ounce of water and throw it down in one gulp—like the cowboys in black hats tossed off their whiskey in the old Saturday afternoon horse operas.

The pain begins to ease, the coffee is made so I move into the garden room and pick up my laptop computer to record my feelings for "Legacy."

Today is one of those nice autumn days when it would be a great to walk with the puppies over the pastures, through the woods, and along the streams, but those days are gone for me. Now Miss Beth brings the puppies inside for an hour or two a couple of times each day. Buster is a house dog, but spends most of his day outside with Spanky. When Buster is in the house without Spanky he's usually well behaved, but Spanky is still a wild outdoor kind of dog and after they have been in the house together, it looks like a tornado touched down … but Miss Beth has all the patience in the world. She takes them back to their run and straightens up the mess the tornado left behind. Since Mohammed can no longer go to the mountain, Miss Beth brings the mountain to Mohammed. She does all this extra work so that Spanky, Buster and I can spend some time together. In my world this is called devotion.

It would be much more fun to play outside with the puppies, but that will not be again so it's important to find a substitute: Miss Beth is a genius at finding substitute activities to replace the ones I am giving up, as physical limitations continue to creep into my life.

I feel better this morning than I have in several days. The days and especially the nights are getting cooler now. It was pleasant to wake up this morning to sixty-two degree temperatures. Last evening at twilight Miss Beth and I were able to sit outside and talk. It was almost cool enough to put on a light sweater with a nice breeze blowing.

We have had a brutal summer. We had one five-consecutive-day period when the temperature was topped three digits. One day it was one hundred-five, two days it was one hundred-four and two days an even one hundred. It broke records each of those five days. We also had several more days of more than one hundred degrees this August, and we didn't have a single day in August when the temperature was less than ninety degrees. To add insult to injury, we hardly had enough rain to measure during July and August.

I've missed gardening. This is the first year in many years that I haven't spent most of my days in the garden during all of the seasons. I often sit in the garden room and watch Miss Beth as she prunes, dead heads, and weeds, and the young man we have hired to help her mows, trims, and blows. I sit and watch them and I cry. I cry because I so miss being able to do those things.

I don't think much about the cancer that is eating away at my bones, but I do think a lot about the things it is causing me to miss. I miss walking with Miss Beth and the dogs especially on cool fall mornings and we are almost on that season now. I miss just being outside with the dogs in their run. I miss being able to walk down to the big spring and watch the cool clear water bubble out of the rocks

I've had a good life. I would like to see it continue for another few years, but that's not my call. It looks as though I may get a few more months, so I'll do everything in my power to make them the best few months of the seventy-five years I've had so far.

I started life on a small farm in Alabama at the foot of the Great Appalachian Mountain chain. The highest peak in Alabama is Cheaha Mountain. It's the beginning of the southern end of the Appalachian chain. On a clear day we could see the great mountains if we went just up the road a piece from Mr. Willie and Miss Emily's little farm where I spent a lot of time during my growing up years.

My plans are for my life to end on The Blessed Earth Farm. On a clear day if I go a mile or two down Green Pond Road, I can see the great mountain chain. These are the same mountains I saw as a boy on that other little farm, but I'm a couple of hundred miles northeast of where I was then. It seems kind of strange that I started out on a little farm where life was lived about as simple as life can be lived and that, if my plans and wishes are fulfilled, I'll end life on a little farm where life is lived about as simple as life can be lived in our complex society of today. In between, especially the years from when I was twenty years old to the fifty-sixth year, my life was about as complex with social and business affairs as life gets. So, I can say that I've lived life both ways and, for me, simple is definitely better.

Now the moments of life grow precious. I still feel as I have all along that death is a part of living. I've had many discussions with a lot of people since my death sentence was pronounced last December. Miss Beth and I agreed that we would openly talk about my death, believing that it would help. It has helped us; I think we both have positioned ourselves to accept that my death is near, and we will face it hand-in-hand as we have other tribulations in our marriage.

The thing that has surprised me most is that almost everyone has a problem talking about imminent death, even many medical and social professionals who deal with it everyday. I don't know why this is so. We've all had death in our lives. We know people die. Perhaps the reason we have trouble talking about it is that, although we know that everyone dies, if we don't talk about it maybe we won't die.

My five children had a lot of trouble talking about my death in the beginning, but after months of talking to them individually, I think they are now fairly comfortable talking about it. In the beginning when I asked them why they had so much trouble talking about me dying, they didn't have an answer to the question. They are now able to tell me that it is because it will leave a big hole in their lives, and they aren't quite ready to face that yet.

I know from personal experience that this is true. Death has taken my first wife, my mother, my father, my brother, and one of my children, and each did leave a big hole in my life. My father died at forty-one, I was nineteen and there have been so many times as I faced the problems of life, and raising a family, that I wanted him to lean on and to provide advice. My mother died when she was seventy-six and I was fifty-six. No matter how old one is when they lose their mother, there is always a huge black hole left in one's life. My brother died when he was sixty-seven and I was seventy. We were close all our lives and his death left a hole in my life also. I remember us as boys playing and fighting and doing all the things brothers who are close do as they grow up together.

I think the most surprising thing is the big hole I still feel about losing an infant daughter. Her name was Linda Kay, and she only lived three days, but in those three days I got to hold her and I loved her. You never have to learn to love your child. It comes naturally the moment you first see them. I never talk about it to anyone, but there is seldom a day that goes by that I don't think of her. There is really no one to talk to about her; she was our first, so none of her siblings ever knew her. Her mother and grandparents are now dead, but for a while longer there's still me to remember her.

She would have been fifty-five last July. I wonder what kind of woman she would have grown up to become. She could have children and grandchildren by now. She could be congresswoman or a senator, or she could be a famous author, or she could be a contented woman who has raised her family and is now living in peace, on a little farm in the shadows of the great mountains somewhere. I think of her everyday and I wonder. I'm the only one alive today who knew her, and I shall soon be gone also. Who will remember her then?

It's Sunday morning and about an hour ago, about ten-thirty this morning Miss Beth interrupted my writing and newspaper reading—I've been alternating between the two since about six o'clock this morning—and asked if I would like to take a break and ride my electric scooter down to the barn, get out the Gator and go for a ride. It's a cool, bordering-on-fall morning, so I decided she had had another of her many good ideas. The top speed on the Gator is about twenty-five miles an hour and more realistically the cruising speed is about fifteen miles an hour. It's good that we live in a remote area, or all those folks out there, who haven't yet learned not to hurry, would have been driving their cars on our rear bumper, blowing horns, and giving us the finger, because we're making them late to church. As it was, we rode the country roads for several miles and only saw two cars. It's great living in the country.

I have a beautiful place to die. I guess for the last couple of weeks before my death that it won't matter, I'll likely be in a coma, but until then I will enjoy every precious moment of our garden room and The Blessed Earth Farm, and the beauty with which Miss Beth surrounds me.

Miss Beth and I have lived on The Blessed Earth Farm for nine years and eighteen days today. I've lived here longer, but I'm going to do my best to make it an even ten years for the two of us. We've made it into the kind of place in which we've always wanted to live. We've made about two acres of ornamental gardens around the house, and built onto the house to suit our needs. Our greatest addition to the house was the garden room. We knocked out the dining room wall and built a room twenty-two feet by fifteen feet; it's all glass including the roof. All you see in the room is glass, cedar and Italian floor tile, and outside you can see even beyond the gardens to hay fields, pastures and woods.

The room looks out on most of the gardens. It's like you're sitting out in the garden, but are protected from the elements. I love to sit in the room and watch the storm clouds gather and the lightning flash, and listen to the thunder roar. The best thing though is when the rain starts. A lot of folks today haven't heard the sound of rain on the tin roof of a room with no ceilings, just the rafters and the tin between you and the elements. That's what the rain sounds like on our glass roof. We, however, have the added benefit of looking up and *seeing* the rain run down the roof to be carried away by the gutters.

At night I turn out all the lights and sit in the garden room, looking up at the stars and the old man in the moon—if he isn't too lazy to get up on that particular night. I love to sit in the room and read at twilight. The light is just right for reading and it makes me feel as though I am sitting on a mountain top after a hard day of backpacking, catching the last rays of light to read by before time to climb into the sleeping bag and watch the dying fire.

I sleep in my recliner in the garden room a good bit now. It's a good change from the bed. Both are important in that they give me the change in positions that my body so badly needs, yet can't achieve by changing positions in the bed, because there are several pain areas in my body where the pressure of lying on them is just too much. It's nice to wake up in the garden room and look up at the stars and then drift back to sleep

Miss Beth has spent many hours this summer planting colorfully blooming perennials around the garden room, and lugging huge pots of roses, saliva, sages, moss rose, chrysanthemums, and many more onto the deck off of the garden room, so that I can see the brilliant blooms and smell the fragrance of the sages, as I can no longer walk the gardens. She has practically surrounded the hot tub with these fragrant plants, which adds so much to the enjoyable experience of soaking in the tub. Miss Beth has also kept gardenias sitting by my recliner in the garden room almost all summer, so that I have the company of their fragrance. She not only says she loves me, she proves it by all the things she does for me.

It's October. I've written several times in this book that my two favorite months of the year are October and April. It's looks as though I'm going to get to see my beautiful October blue sky and gold light once again. Maybe I'll even feel like riding some of the mountain roads in the convertible with the top down. The leaves are beautiful from the convertible, because you can not only look out at them, but you can look straight up at them. I'll miss being able to drive. Driving a convertible on winding mountain roads is one of my favorite things to do. With Miss Beth doing the driving, however, I can do more sight seeing.

April is the month of my birthday. Perhaps I'll live to see one more soft April and my seventy-sixth birthday. If I can do that I'll get to see the daffodils bloom once again.

I don't know what happens from here. I know I want to try to make my death as easy for those who love me, and as easy for myself as possible. Other than that, I guess I'll just take it day by day. People have talked to me a lot about what happens after death. I don't know. My spiritual beliefs borrow from the philosophy of many religions, even agnostics, but embrace none of them. I have requested that my body be cremated and its ashes strewn over the gardens of The Blessed Earth Farm.

There's a little poem I've had for years. I don't remember where I got it and I don't know who wrote it because the author is listed as unknown. It expresses my thoughts on this subject well:

> Do not stand at my grave and weep,
> I am not there,
> I do not sleep.
> I am a thousand winds that blow;
> I am the diamond glints on the snow.
> I am the sunlight on ripened grain;
> I am the gentle autumn's rain.
> When you awaken in the morning's hush,
> I am the swift uplifting rush
> Of quiet birds in circled flight.
> I am the soft star that shines at night.
> Do not stand at my grave and cry.
> I am not there; I did not die.
> *Author Unknown*

About the Author

Winston Hardegree, Master Gardener, spent the past twenty years gardening, writing, teaching Master Gardener classes, and volunteering with various community organizations, including Habitat for Humanity. Winston was a high-level executive of an international textile company before leaving that hectic world for a simpler life in rural South Carolina.

978-0-595-71443-8
0-595-71443-9

Printed in the United States
99492LV00005B/83/A